Glimpses of the Christ

Sermons from the Gospels

JARL K. WAGGONER

EDITOR

JAMES P. COFFEY

ASSOCIATE EDITOR

GLIMPSES OF THE CHRIST:
Sermons from the Gospels

Kainos Books
Waxhaw, North Carolina
kainosbooks.com

ISBN – 13: 978-0615919423

Cover: A gathering storm on the Sea of Galilee.
Photo courtesy of Reed Waggoner.

The contributors dedicate this book to the memory of the following colleagues and classmates, who faithfully labored in the work of the gospel till the day they were promoted to glory.

S. Herbert Bess	James L. Boyer
Herman Hoyt	Ted Legg
David Plaster	Tom Sharp
Charles R. Smith	Bob Wiedeman

Contents

Preface

Some years ago I visited the Boston Public Library, the oldest public library in the United States. On display in the archives room at that time were some of the first books brought to the American shores, as well as some of the first books published in the Colonies. Given our country's rich Christian history, I was not surprised to see many books (maybe the majority) that were explicitly Christian in nature. There were many Bibles, of course, as well as many hymnals. And somewhat to my surprise, there were also a large number of sermon collections. In fact, it struck me that the sermon collections seemed to outnumber strictly theological works.

Upon reflection, however, I recalled that it was sermons that God the Holy Spirit used to initiate the First Great Awakening. Yes, those sermons grew out of serious theological study and understanding—just read Jonathan Edwards, for example—but sermons were the means of spiritual awakening. And why should we be surprised by this? Sermons are what communicate the great theological truths to the masses. They are the means of urging acceptance and compliance with the demands of Scripture—and this has not changed! Even in an era when sermons too often have been replaced with "conversations" and watered-down snippets designed to appeal to an impatient, make-it-easy culture in which the word *commitment* raises eyebrows as if it were foreign to our language, sermons—biblical, passionate, powerful sermons—are still the primary means God uses to convert, teach, and equip people to live the God-honoring lives He intended us all to live.

This collection of sermons from the Gospels serves several purposes. First, it gives voice to some of America's finest expository preachers. Readers may not be familiar with all the names, but they represent a host of preachers who are carrying on the art of biblical preaching in countless churches in the United States.

Second, to readers who may not be familiar with preaching that accurately explains and applies the Bible, this book serves as an introduction. Too many hear messages about the Bible rather than hearing for themselves what the Bible teaches. Hopefully, this book will challenge such readers to seek out churches, preachers, and ministries that focus on the Bible, which "is inspired by God and profitable for teaching, for reproof, for correction, for training in righteousness; so that the man of God may be adequate, equipped for every good work" (2 Tim. 3:16-17).

Third, these sermons serve as examples to young pastors or pastors-in-training of the kind of preaching that needs to be practiced faithfully in our churches, today and in the future. Readers will find variety in style and approach in these sermons, and that is as it should be. But they will also find consistency in bringing forth the accurate meaning of Scripture in a way that touches people where they live. Truth is always practical, and those whose sermons are included here are committed to disseminating the truth of the Bible without compromise. As such, their sermons provide fine examples for young preachers to follow.

Fourth, the sermons in this book are all from the New Testament Gospels, which focus on the life and teaching and works of our Lord Jesus Christ. He is God in the flesh, the Creator, Redeemer, Savior, and Lord. He is central to all of history and the center of all the Bible. To study any portion of the life of Christ is a worthy pursuit that can only benefit us. If these sermons serve no other purpose than giving readers a greater understanding of, appreciation for, and commitment to Jesus Christ, they will have accomplished as much or more than the contributors ever could have hoped for.

The sermons in this volume come from all areas of Christ's life. They are not comprehensive by any means but are representative glimpses of Christ's life. All the contributors are graduates of Grace Theological Seminary in Winona Lake, Indiana.[1] They represent various churches, schools, and ministries and several generations, yet the training they hold in common brings a theological consistency to the sermons. Also, interspersed among the sermons are several

---

[1] Grace Theological Seminary itself had no part in the production and publishing of this book.

charts and topical essays that contribute to the big picture of the Gospels.

On behalf of all who contributed to this book, I trust that the preaching of Christ herein will in some part accomplish the great work of "admonishing every man and teaching every man with all wisdom, so that we may present every man complete in Christ" (Col. 1:28).

Jarl K. Waggoner

Contributors

JAMES P. COFFEY trusted the Lord Jesus Christ as his Savior in July 1973. He graduated from Mercer University with a Bachelor of Arts in History and Art. James earned his Education Certificate from Grace College and graduated from Grace Theological Seminary with a Certificate in Biblical Studies. He taught English as a Second Language in Knoxville, Tennessee, and regularly wrote "The Jewish Aspect" for *The Bible Expositor and Illuminator*. He currently lives in Atlanta, Georgia, with his wife Debra.

LEE COMPSON is a native of Warsaw, Indiana. He received a degree in youth ministry from Grace College before moving on to Grace Theological Seminary, where he completed his Master of Divinity. Soon after, he married Stephanie (Moore), whom he had met in college, and they settled down in Winona Lake, where they both worked. In addition to his "normal" job, Lee continued to serve in his home church, leading the college and young adult ministry, which he had overseen since college. In January 2013, he became senior pastor at Milford First Brethren Church in Milford, Indiana. Lee is an avid sports fan and enjoys playing basketball and slow-pitch softball in his spare time.

IVAN FRENCH served three churches before returning to his alma mater, Grace Theological Seminary, where he taught for over twenty years. Known for his warm heart and humorous stories (what he called "illustrative anecdotes"), he taught Bible, theology, and church history with both an academic knowledge and practical application. His teaching infused a heart and energy for Christ and the church in the seminary program. During this time he continued to be active in pastoral ministry, campus leadership, global missions, and Bible conferences, encouraging and strengthening the men and women he had helped to train. Ivan and his wife Arloeen are now retired and live in Winona Lake, Indiana.

JOHN FRENCH serves as site director for Grace College, Fort Wayne (ftw.grace.edu). He has been a pastor, teacher, and administrator, with twenty-five years of experience in church planting, leadership development, and higher education in Johannesburg, South Africa, and the USA. He is a graduate of Moody Bible Institute, Grace College and Seminary, and the University of South Africa. He enjoys travel, reading, jogging, cricket (that's a sport), and music. He and his wife, Christine, have a married daughter and a teenage son.

ERNIE GODSHALL is a graduate of Bob Jones University and Grace Theological Seminary and holds a Doctor of Ministry degree from Westminster Seminary. He served as a pastor in North Vernon, Indiana, from 1978 to 1991. Since 1992 he has been senior pastor of Faith Bible Church in Evansville, Indiana. He and his wife reside in Newburgh, Indiana. They have three children and eight grand-children.

ISAAC (IKE) GRAHAM has been senior pastor of the Orrville Grace Brethren Church in Orrville, Ohio, since 2000. He also helped to plant the church from 1981 to 1982. He has a Master of Theology degree from Grace Theological Seminary in Winona Lake, Indiana. He served with his wife, Nancy, and their children as missionaries in Japan from 1984 to 1992 under Grace Brethren Foreign Missions and under the Conservative Grace Brethren Churches from 1993 to 1994. He and Nancy have four biological children (Ben, Seth, Rachel, and Joel) and three adopted boys (Arthur, Jessey, and Nathan). He enjoys playing golf.

MICHAEL HONTZ resides in Warsaw, Indiana, along with his wife Marta and their two daughters, Elliana and Emily. After graduating with a B.A. in Bible Theology from Appalachian Bible College, Mike served as a youth pastor in Pennsylvania for four years before moving to Indiana to attend Grace Theological Seminary, where he received the M. Div. in Exegetical Studies. Mike ministered at Pleasant View Bible Church in various pastoral roles before becoming the senior pastor in 2011.

ROBERT B. (BOB) LANNING graduated with an M. Div. from Grace Theological Seminary in 1977 and since then has pastored independent churches, in Newell, Iowa; Manton, Michigan; and currently at

Cornerstone Bible Church in Lancaster, South Carolina. He is a member of the IFCA International, has served on the board of Baptist Haiti Mission, and has been a pastoral advisor to a Michigan chapter of Child Evangelism Fellowship. He and his wife Nancy have been blessed with four children and twelve grandchildren.

RICHARD L. MAYHUE is executive vice president and dean of The Master's Seminary. He is a graduate of Ohio State University and received his M.Div., Th.M., and Th.D. degrees from Grace Theological Seminary. From 1977 to 1980 he taught in the areas of New Testament and Pastoral Ministries at the seminary before joining the pastoral staff of Grace Community Church under Dr. John MacArthur. Dr. Mayhue served as senior pastor of the Grace Brethren Church of Long Beach, California from 1984 to 1989 and then joined the faculty of The Master's Seminary. He has authored, contributed to, and/or edited, over thirty books, including *How To Interpret the Bible for Yourself*, *The Healing Promise*, *What Would Jesus Say About Your Church?*, *Seeking God*, *Practicing Proverbs*, *Unmasking Satan*, *1 & 2 Thessalonians*, *Bible Boot Camp*, and *Christ's Prophetic Plans*.

TOM TRIGGS earned the B.A. in Bible from Grace College, and the Diploma in Theology and M.A. in Ministry from Grace Theological Seminary, as well as a Ph.D. in apologetics. He served twenty-four years in pastoral ministry in Indiana, Illinois, and Ohio and also taught for seven years in Grace College's prison extension program. He is presently the head of Make a Defense Creation Ministries (www.make-a-defense.org).

JARL K. WAGGONER is a professional writer, editor, and publisher. He is the author of *Prophets for Our Time: An Exposition of Obadiah and Jonah* (Wipf and Stock) and *The World's Views: A Christian Perspective on the Beliefs of Our Day* (Kainos). His published writings number in the hundreds and include magazine articles, reviews, and Sunday school lessons, as well as a popular baseball quiz book. He has served as an associate pastor and currently is managing editor of the *Creation Research Society Quarterly*. He is a graduate of Marietta College and Grace Theological Seminary. He and his wife Winona, also a Grace Seminary graduate, have five children.

JOHN C. WHITCOMB is a scholar, teacher, author, and lecturer. He received degrees from Princeton University (B.A.) and Grace Theological Seminary (B.D., Th.M., Th.D.) and served for thirty-eight years as professor of Old Testament and Christian theology at Grace. He has authored numerous books on biblical creation, including *The Genesis Flood* (with Henry Morris), *The Early Earth,* and *The World That Perished,* along with commentaries on the Old Testament books of Ezra, Nehemiah, Esther, Daniel, Kings, and Chronicles. His latest book, *The Rapture and Beyond,* is a study of the end times. Dr. Whitcomb currently serves as president of Whitcomb Ministries (www.whitcombministries.org).

*****

Editor
JARL K. WAGGONER (see above)

Associate Editor
JAMES P. COFFEY (see above)

Proofreader
WINONA M. WAGGONER graduated from Arizona College of the Bible (B.A.) and Grace Theological Seminary (M.A. Missions) and received training in proofreading at Graduate School USA. She grew up on the mission field in South America and has been involved in missions in the South Pacific and in the Ukraine. She is the mother of four boys and a girl and currently serves at the JAARS Center in Waxhaw, North Carolina, as supervisor of Penn Lodge.

1

Human Dilemmas—Heavenly Answers

(Matthew 1:18-25)

JARL K. WAGGONER

My daughter's youth choir moved on to the next house on the block, bringing their beautiful carols to the winter evening. To the door came a mother and two small boys. They listened and expressed their delight in the choir's performance. When the choir director asked if there was any particular song they would like to hear, one of the boys piped up with his suggestion: "Take Me Out to the Ball Game." It wasn't exactly a Christmas carol, but the choir obliged.

We laugh at how children sometimes can be so unaware of things. Yet adults too can seem utterly clueless at times—even about things of great importance. For most people the focus of Christmas is on buying and giving and receiving with perhaps a little goodwill thrown in. And even Christians can get a bit sidetracked by holiday activities. Sometimes the events at Bethlehem so long ago become no more than cold facts that are not fully appreciated.

As we look at Matthew's account of Jesus' birth, we want to enter the human drama of Joseph and dwell on the unique work of God in the incarnation. At Bethlehem the concerns of man and the work of God meet in the God-Man born there.

A Disappointing Dilemma (Matt. 1:18-19)

> *18 Now the birth of Jesus Christ was as follows: when His mother Mary had been betrothed to Joseph, before they came together she was found to be with*

child by the Holy Spirit. [19] *And Joseph her husband,*
being a righteous man and not wanting to disgrace
her, planned to send her away secretly.

Matthew sets forth the background of Jesus Christ first through His genealogy (vv. 1-17) and then through the details of His birth (vv. 18-25). Concerning His birth, Matthew begins "when His mother Mary had been betrothed to Joseph." We may think of betrothal, or espousal, as similar to what we call engagement today. However, in the Jewish custom, betrothal was legally binding. A pledge was taken before witnesses, and, although they had not come together to live as a married couple, they were considered as husband and wife from that point on. Note that Joseph is, in fact, called Mary's "husband" in verse 19. To break an engagement today might bring awkwardness, embarrassment, or even bitterness. To break a betrothal in Joseph and Mary's time required legal action—essentially a "divorce"—and infidelity during the time of betrothal was considered "adultery."[1]

Before the marriage itself took place, Mary "was found to be with child." Matthew adds "by the Holy Spirit," which assumes a knowledge of the Luke 1 account of Mary's conception by the work of God the Holy Spirit. Mary, of course, knew the source of her pregnancy (Luke 1:31-38), but apparently she remained silent about it, allowing God to deal with a situation that would only be exacerbated by her pleas of innocence.

With the discovery of Mary's pregnancy before their marriage, Joseph faced a dilemma. A marriage potentially can withstand infidelity; a betrothal could not. If one of the parties proved even before marriage he or she couldn't be trusted, there was not much hope for the marriage. Joseph had two choices: He could present a public accusation against Mary and perhaps demand punishment;[2]

---

[1] Robert H. Stein, *Luke,* The New American Commentary (Nashville: Broadman, 1992), 82.

[2] Under the Old Testament law, adultery, as this was considered, could be punished by death (Deut. 22:23-24), though it is doubtful this was ever widely practiced and almost certainly not in Joseph's time. See William Hendriksen, *The*

or he could choose to "send her away secretly," that is, contractually "divorce" her. So it was that Joseph faced a dilemma. He was confronted with a difficult decision and, seemingly, had no good choice.

Joseph, however, was "a righteous man" and didn't want to "disgrace her." He was desirous of pleasing God but in a way that did not unduly put Mary "to open shame," as the word is translated in Hebrews 6:6. There was no way for Mary to completely escape shame, but Joseph was unwilling to add to it; so he planned to end the betrothal as quietly as possible.

A Unique Answer (Matt. 1:20-23)

> [20] *But when he had considered this, behold, an angel of the Lord appeared to him in a dream, saying, "Joseph, son of David, do not be afraid to take Mary as your wife; for the Child who has been conceived in her is of the Holy Spirit.* [21] *She will bear a Son; and you shall call His name Jesus, for He will save His people from their sins."* [22] *Now all this took place to fulfill what was spoken by the Lord through the prophet:* [23] *"BEHOLD, THE VIRGIN SHALL BE WITH CHILD AND SHALL BEAR A SON, AND THEY SHALL CALL HIS NAME IMMANUEL," which translated means, "GOD WITH US."*

Dilemmas exist only with humans. There are no dilemmas with God, and there would be none for us if we possessed God's knowledge and insight. In these verses (20-23) we find God's answer to Joseph's dilemma. It is a revelation to us for sure, but it was revealed specifically to Joseph to answer his concerns.

A Unique Conception (v. 20)

When Joseph had considered his options and decided on the one that caused the least public embarrassment for both Mary and

---

Gospel of Matthew, New Testament Commentary (Grand Rapids: Baker, 1973), 130.

him, "an angel" appeared to him in a dream. An angel had spoken directly to Mary (Luke 1:26-38), but an angel spoke to Joseph in a dream, as was the case on other occasions with Joseph (Matt. 2:13, 19, 22) and the wise men (Matt. 2:12). The angel addressed Joseph as "son of David." This was a reminder to Joseph of his Davidic ancestry, which was also the ancestry of the Messiah (Matt. 1:1). In almost all other uses in the Gospels, the term is used as a title for the Messiah, Jesus Christ.

The angel's message to Joseph was, "Do not be afraid to take Mary as your wife." Though it would go against custom and require much of both Joseph and Mary, Joseph was to proceed with the marriage. He had nothing to fear regarding Mary's character or actions, for the Child she carried had been conceived by the Holy Spirit. No explanation was given about how this could be, and indeed there was no explanation: it was a miracle. We often speak of the miraculous "virgin birth," but the birth of Jesus was not itself a miracle but presumably a normal, human birth. It was the *conception* of Jesus in the body of Mary that was the true miracle.

A Unique Role (v. 21)

The angel went on to inform Joseph that Mary's Child would be a son and that Joseph was to name him Jesus (v. 21). *Jesus* means "the Lord is salvation." The name was not unique. It was the Greek equivalent of the Hebrew Joshua, or Yeshua. However, the Child was uniquely named. In fact, both Mary (Luke 1:31) and Joseph were told to give Him this name, though only Joseph was told the reason: "He will save His people from their sins." Clearly, it was important that His name be connected to His unique, divine work of salvation. That work would be extended to all people, but it was in fulfillment of promises made to "His people," the Jews.

This Child, Jesus, would be *the* Savior. But unlike the saviors, or deliverers, of the Old Testament era, particularly the judges (cf. 2 Kings 13:5; Neh. 9:27; Obad. 21), He would save people from their sins—that is, from the corruption, consequences, and slavery of sin. John the Baptist introduced Him as "the Lamb of God who takes away the sin of the world" (John 1:29), and Jesus understood clearly that His purpose in coming into the world was to "seek and to save that which was lost" (Luke 19:10). Joseph surely recognized, as Mary did (Luke 1:32-33), that Mary's Child was the long-awaited Messiah (Christ) of Israel, the Deliverer who would free His people, not from physical enemies, but from the spiritual enemy and slave-master known as sin.

A Unique Person (vv. 22-23)

It is unclear whether the words recorded in verses 22-23 were spoken by the angel or were the author Matthew's commentary. In either case, they were divinely inspired words affirming that the miraculous conception that had transpired was in fulfillment of Isaiah's prophecy of the virgin birth. That prophecy in Isaiah 7:14 is quoted in verse 23. There is much debate about Isaiah's prophecy on two fronts. First, there is the question regarding the translation of the Hebrew word rendered "virgin" in Isaiah and whether it could, or should, be understood simply as "young woman of marriageable age." While "virgin" is certainly a good translation of the Hebrew term, whatever ambiguity might exist in the word's meaning is removed by Matthew's translation, which uses the Greek word *parthenos,* which can mean only "virgin."[3]

The second question concerns whether there was a double fulfillment of the prophecy, first in Isaiah's day and then later in the birth of Jesus. This is something the apostle Matthew did not hint at and certainly did not discuss. His concern was to point out that the conception and birth of the Savior was a clear fulfillment of what Isaiah had prophesied seven centuries earlier.[4] In so doing, Matthew was establishing not only the truth of the virgin birth as Luke did, but also the scriptural credentials of Israel's Messiah. There could be no doubt as to Jesus' identity.

---

[3] *Parthenos* is also the word used in the Septuagint, or Greek translation, of Isaiah 7:14.

[4] For more detailed discussions of the Isaiah prophecy in relation to Christ, see Hendriksen, *Matthew,* 133-45; Robert Glenn Gromacki, *The Virgin Birth: Doctrine of Deity* (Nashville: Nelson, 1974), esp. chapter 7; and Edward E. Hindson, *Isaiah's Immanuel* (Philadelphia: Presbyterian and Reformed, 1978).

The latter part of Isaiah's prophecy states of the Child born of the virgin, "They shall call His name Immanuel." Matthew adds the meaning of this name: "God with us." This Child was also "God with us," the God-Man. Such a name in its fullest meaning could be applied only to Christ. Yet in the New Testament Immanuel was never used as a name for Jesus. This suggests that it was not a title but rather a characterization or description of Jesus. As such, it was almost equivalent to "Son of God." The term emphasizes that He is both God and man, and this is what allowed Him to be our Savior. As God He could provide the perfect, sinless offering for our sin; and as man He could suffer the punishment for our sins.

A Faithful Response (Matt. 1:24-25)

> [24] *And Joseph awoke from his sleep and did as the angel of the Lord commanded him, and took Mary as his wife, [25] but kept her a virgin until she gave birth to a Son; and he called His name Jesus.*

Joseph had seen none of this; God had to reveal it to him. And while much of this remained a mystery to him, Joseph's decision was now clear-cut. His was no longer a choice between two bad options; it was a choice between obeying and following the Lord and not doing so. That didn't mean his decision was easy. After all, Joseph could have spared himself much grief, outwardly at least, by walking away from Mary. By walking away, Mary would have borne shame, suspicion, ridicule, and ostracism. By taking her as his wife, Joseph would bear much of that himself. Unlike our traditions, it was the groom, not the bride, who was the focus of the ancient Israelite wedding—and the wedding feast lasted seven days. To go through with all this would draw plenty of attention to Joseph, and much of it would be unwelcomed attention.

Joseph, however, was obedient to the angelic message and "took Mary as his wife." He followed through with the marriage, but we are told he "kept her a virgin until she gave birth." There is no indication he was explicitly told to do this, but this enabled the couple to refute every allegation that Joseph was Jesus' human father.

Conclusion

In this life we sometimes face dilemmas, simply because we are finite and not omniscient. We long to know what road to take, what is the course of righteousness. In those times we can turn again to God's Word for guidance, and we can accept God's invitation to ask Him for wisdom (James 1:5).

Unbelievers face a dilemma far greater than anything we might confront. They know there is a God, even if they suppress the knowledge of Him (Rom. 1:18-20). They know God exists, and they want to be free of His constraints; and yet they long to find purpose in their lives.

All these dilemmas bring us back to Bethlehem. Ultimately, it is there that all our doubts, concerns, and dilemmas find their answer. The answer is in the unique Person born into the world there—the God-Man, who came to bring salvation. And who He is—the Mighty God, the Eternal Father, the Prince of Peace (Isa. 9:6)—is proved and preserved by His unique, miraculous conception.

The True Message of Christmas[1]

JOHN C. WHITCOMB

Every year it becomes sadly apparent that fewer and fewer Americans understand what Christmas really means. Christmas is an international celebration of a moment in history on planet Earth when God's eternal Son, whom we know as the Lord Jesus Christ, became a genuine and permanent member of mankind in order to die for our sins upon a cross.

The key word is *love*—not our love but God's love. In spite of our profound selfishness, pride, and indifference to the claims of a holy and loving God, He—not willing that any should perish—provided the perfect sacrifice, the Lamb of God, to die in our place, as our substitute, our divine and sinless representative, and to rise from the dead.

Christ (the Messiah) was born in Bethlehem of Judea and raised in Nazareth of Galilee two thousand years ago. He was sent into the world by God the Father because of the Father's love for human beings.

A brilliant, God-honoring medical doctor and historian named Luke described what happened one night in the city of Nazareth. An angel came to a young Jewish woman named Mary and announced, "The Holy Spirit will come upon you, and the power of the Most High will overshadow you; and for that reason the holy Child shall be called the Son of God" (Luke 1:35).

What does this mean? A miracle of cosmic magnitude was about to occur. That is why this messenger from God explained, "For nothing will be impossible with God" (Luke 1:37). Jeremiah had used this same expression six hundred years earlier when contemplating the creation of the universe: "Ah Lord GOD! Behold, You

---

have made the heavens and the earth by Your great power… Nothing is too difficult for You" (Jer. 32:17).

But how could the Son of God, the Second Person of the triune Godhead, add a human nature to His eternal, divine nature without becoming two persons and without the human person being not only finite but also sinful?

The Holy Spirit solved this dilemma by using the genetic information in the body of the Jewish virgin, wholly apart from the function of a human father and to the exclusion of her sin nature. (See Luke 1:47, where Mary stated that God was her Savior, as proof that Mary had a sin nature.)

Note the special emphasis: "The Holy Spirit will come upon you, and the power of the Most High will overshadow you" (Luke 1:35a). It is only for this reason that she could be assured "the holy Child shall be called the Son of God" (v. 35b).

The preexistent, divine Person, who was the Son of God, assumed a human *nature* through Mary, but not a human *person*. He became one Person with two natures—the divine nature dominating the human nature without in any way canceling its nonglorified limitations, such as limited knowledge (Luke 2:52), weariness (John 4:6), hunger (Mark 11:12) and thirst (John 19:28). In fact, He was "tempted in all things as we are, yet without sin" (Heb. 4:15).

Thus, the incomparable miracle of divine incarnation by means of virgin conception resulted in a Person who is not only 100 percent deity but also a 100-percent descendant of David (Matt. 1:1; Rev. 5:5; 22:16), Judah (Heb. 7:14), Abraham (Matt. 1:1), and Adam (Luke 3:38). It was not a mere theophany, an appearance of humanity, that died on the cross. It was a genuine and sinless human being who bore our sins and served as our perfect Substitute.

The author of Hebrews expressed the Christmas message in a marvelously precise way: "Therefore, since the children share in flesh and blood, He Himself likewise also partook of the same, that through death He might render powerless him who had the power of death, that is, the devil, and might free those who through fear of death were subject to slavery all their lives. For assuredly He does not give help to angels, but He gives help to the descendant of Abraham. Therefore, He had to be made like His brethren in all things, so that He might become a merciful and faithful high priest in things pertaining to God, to make propitiation for the sins of the people" (Heb. 2:14-17).

Thank God for the true message of Christmas!

2

The Temptation of Jesus

(Matthew 4:1-10)

JOHN FRENCH

Have you heard the folk story of the bandit José Rivera, who became notorious in several little towns in Texas for robbing their banks and businesses? Finally, the townsfolk, weary of the constant plundering, hired a ranger to track down José Rivera in his hideout in Mexico and retrieve the stolen money. The ranger at last arrived at a desolate, ramshackle cantina. At the counter he saw a young man enjoying his brew. At one of the tables, hands over his ample stomach and hat over his eyes, snored another patron. With much gusto, the ranger approached the young man at the bar and announced that he was on a mission to bring back José Rivera, dead or alive. "Can you help me find him?" he asked. The young man smiled, pointed to the other patron, and said, "That is José Rivera."

The ranger ambled over to the sleeping bandit. He tapped the man on the shoulder and asked, "Are you José Rivera?" The man mumbled, "No speak English." The ranger beckoned to the young man to help him communicate his mission.

The ensuing conversation was tedious. First, the ranger spoke in English, and the young man translated it into Spanish. José Rivera responded in Spanish, and the young man repeated the answer in English for the ranger.

Finally, the ranger warned José Rivera that he had two choices. He could tell the ranger where all the loot he had stolen was hidden, in which case he could walk away a free man; or, if he refused to reveal where the money was stashed, he would be shot dead instantly. The young man translated the ultimatum.

José Rivera pulled himself together and said to the young man, "Tell the ranger to go out of the bar, turn to the right, and go about a mile. He will see a well. Near the well he will see a very tall tree. Beside the trunk of that tree is a large concrete slab. He will need help in removing it. Under the slab is a pit in the ground. If he carefully uncovers it, he will find all the jewelry and most of the money I have taken."

The young man turned to the ranger, opened his mouth, swallowed, paused, and then said, "José Rivera says—José Rivera says, 'Go ahead and shoot!'"[1]

Temptation is a part of life; indeed, it is a part of the *Christian* life. In English to *tempt* means "to entice to sin." The Bible word, however, also can mean "to test." Certainly, Satan desired to cause Jesus to sin. But viewed from God's perspective, it is probably better to understand the temptation of Jesus in Matthew 4[2] as tests that strengthened Jesus' commitment to the will of His Father (cf. James 1:13). In Jesus' victory over Satan, we have a pattern for resisting temptation in the spiritual conflicts of our own lives. Notice the three kinds of temptation that Jesus faced.

Temptation of Substitutes (Matt. 4:1-4)

> [1] *Then Jesus was led up by the Spirit into the wilderness to be tempted by the devil.* [2] *And after He had fasted forty days and forty nights, He then became hungry.* [3] *And the tempter came and said to Him, "If You are the Son of God, command that these stones become bread."* [4] *But He answered and said, "It is written, 'MAN SHALL NOT LIVE ON BREAD ALONE, BUT ON EVERY WORD THAT PROCEEDS OUT OF THE MOUTH OF GOD.'"*

The Temptation

The first temptation appealed to Jesus' need for food. He had been fasting and praying for forty days and nights in preparation for

---

[1] Ravi Zacharias, *Can Man Live Without God?* (Dallas: Word Publishing, 1994), 98-99.

[2] The temptation is also recorded in Mark 1:12-13 and Luke 4:1-13.

His public ministry. He was physically weak and hungry. Satan focused on this need and said, "If You are the Son of God, command that these stones become bread." Satan was asking Jesus to act independently of the Father's will. In other words, he was tempting Jesus to substitute His own will and perspective for the Father's. Remember that Jesus' being in the desert was the will of God (4:1). The Holy Spirit had led Him to this place. By attacking Jesus when He was hungry and tired, Satan was questioning the goodness of God to meet Jesus' needs. He was saying, "If You are the Son of God, You have the power and right to do what You want. So why are You hungry out here? You can do this. You can make these stones into steaming-hot loaves of bread fresh out of the oven."

The Answer

In studying the temptations, it is important not only to hear what Satan suggests, but also to listen to Jesus' reply. For in His replies He gives us insight into the real issue.

Jesus responded to this first temptation with a principle of Scripture. Following their departure from Egypt, the nation of Israel had been in the desert of Sinai for forty years. In Deuteronomy Moses was preparing them for entrance into the Promised Land. God promised to bless them if they trusted and obeyed Him. In fact, their whole experience in the wilderness was meant to show them that God's word was more reliable than their circumstances. The spiritual was more important than the physical. Moses said,

> "He humbled you and let you be hungry, and fed you with manna which you did not know, nor did your fathers know, that He might make you understand that man does not live by bread alone, but man lives by everything that proceeds out of the mouth of the LORD." (Deut. 8:3)

Jesus quoted the last portion of this verse in reply to Satan's temptation. In doing so, He was indicating that it would be wrong for Him to use His divine powers to meet that need outside of the timing and purpose of God.

The Principle

Satan's temptations look most promising when we are tired, confused, or sick. He comes at us when we are vulnerable and worn out. He questions the goodness of God in our circumstances. The temptation is to substitute our desire and way for God's timing and purpose. We must never fulfill a legitimate need in a wrong way. That is, the spiritual must be more important than the physical in our lives.

David had been promised the throne of Israel. As the years dragged on and Saul continually chased him through the deserts of Judah, he had several opportunities to kill Saul and take the throne for himself. His men even urged him to do that: "Look at the opportunity God is giving you." David refused to substitute his legitimate desire for God's timing. "So he said to his men, 'Far be it from me because of the LORD that I should do this thing to my lord, the LORD's anointed, to stretch out my hand against him, since he is the LORD's anointed'" (1 Sam. 24:6).

When we substitute our desires—even good ones—for God's will, we deprive ourselves of the true joys of a righteous and disciplined walk with God. C. S. Lewis said, "We are far too easily pleased."[3] We fill our lives with the passing pleasures of this world so that there is no room for the infinite joy and lasting peace God offers to us in Christ.

Temptation to Test God (Matt. 4:5-7)

> [5] Then the devil took Him into the holy city and had Him stand on the pinnacle of the temple, [6] and said to Him, "If You are the Son of God, throw Yourself down; for it is written, 'HE WILL COMMAND HIS AN-GELS CONCERNING YOU'; and 'ON their HANDS THEY WILL BEAR YOU UP, SO THAT YOU WILL NOT STRIKE

---

[3] C. S. Lewis, *The Weight of Glory and Other Addresses* (Grand Rapids: Eerdmans, 1965), 2.

YOUR FOOT AGAINST A STONE.'" [7] *Jesus said to him,
"On the other hand, it is written, 'YOU SHALL NOT
PUT THE LORD YOUR GOD TO THE TEST.'"*

The Temptation

Satan's second proposal was backed up with a Bible verse. The temple was built on the top of a hill. One corner formed what amounted to a cliff that plunged straight down into the Kidron Valley. I have read estimates that the drop was anywhere from 350 to 450 feet. Somehow Satan transported Jesus to this pinnacle, and there said to Him,

"If You are the Son of God, throw Yourself down; for it is written, 'He will command His angels concerning You'; and 'On their hands they will bear You up, So that You will not strike Your foot against a stone.'"

Satan was quoting Psalm 91:11-12 and in essence saying, "This would be a great way to launch Your messianic career." The Jews, in fact, had a tradition that the Messiah would come to His temple with a display of great power.

The Answer

Jesus again went back to the experience of Israel in the wilderness and quoted these words to Satan: "You shall not put the LORD your God to the test" (Deut. 6:16). Jesus was, in effect, saying, "Yes, God does protect His people, as He promises in the psalm you just misquoted. He will provide for Me. He watches over Me as a Father cares for His son. But I do not have to jump off a skyscraper, or handle snakes, or anything else to prove that God loves Me. When the need arises, He will be there for Me."

The Principle

We are to trust God and His Word rather than test God. But how do we test God?

We test God when we do not believe God in our circumstances. When Israel came out of Egypt, God raised up Moses, sent the ten plagues, opened the Red Sea, and destroyed the army of Pharaoh. Out in the desert they soon became tired, hungry, and thirsty, and

God sent manna to feed them. In Exodus 17 they again had no water, and they began to complain against God and Moses. "Why do you test the LORD?" was Moses' response (17:2). Much of our restless dissatisfaction with life is testing God rather than trusting him.

We test God when we take God's grace for granted. We expect God to treat us with grace while we fail to respect Him and obey Him. Ananias and Sapphira did this. They saw that Barnabas was honored in the church because of his great generosity. So they sold a piece of land and brought the money to the church, pretending that it was the whole amount. Their motive was to get the recognition and praise of the people. After Ananias had been struck down by God in judgment, "Peter *said* to [Sapphira], 'Why is it that you have agreed together to put the Spirit of the Lord to the test? Behold, the feet of those who have buried your husband are at the door, and they will carry you out *as well*'" (Acts 5:9).

I have had people say to me, "I know it's wrong, but God will forgive me." That attitude is testing God rather than trusting him. Someone has wisely said, "You can choose your sin, but you cannot choose your consequences."

We test God when we impose our values on Him. We follow God as we want Him to be rather than for whom He really is. We trust Him when He does what we think He should. We want God simply to be a larger version of us. Patrick Morley warns us that this kind of response leads to cultural Christianity.

> Cultural Christianity means to pursue the God we want instead of the God who is. It is the tendency to be shallow in our understanding of God, wanting Him to be more of a gentle grandfather type who spoils us and lets us have our own way. It is sensing a need for God, but on our own terms. It is wanting the God we have underlined in our Bibles without wanting

the rest of Him, too. It is God relative instead of God absolute.[4]

By all these means, we ask God to prove Himself to us, rather than trust Him by faith.

Temptation of Shortcuts (Matt. 4:8-10)

> [8] *Again, the devil took Him to a very high mountain and showed Him all the kingdoms of the world and their glory;* [9] *and he said to Him, "All these things I will give You, if You fall down and worship me."* [10] *Then Jesus said to him, "Go, Satan! For it is written, 'YOU SHALL WORSHIP THE LORD YOUR GOD, AND SERVE HIM ONLY.'"*

The Temptation

Satan's third temptation appealed to Jesus' mission as Savior and King. He came to redeem the nations of the world. Probably in a vision Satan presented all the nations of the world to Jesus and offered them to Him in exchange for His worship. He showed Jesus the glory and the splendor of these kingdoms. If he were offering the world to Jesus today, he might point out the great medical achievements, the incredible wealth of information and education, the advance of technology, the beauty of the arts, music, and entertainment, the wealth of kings and presidents and the power people of our world, the ease of communication and transportation in the global village, the enjoyment of leisure and tourism, and the beauty of natural resources. Yet at the same time, he would over-look wars, sickness, poverty and hopelessness, AIDS, murder and mayhem, corruption, moral perversions, the slaughter of babies, and the darkness of life without God.

---

[4] Patrick Morley, *The Man in the Mirror: Solving the 24 Problems Men Face* (Grand Rapids: Zondervan, 1997), 53.

31

The Answer

Jesus saw through this false offer. Satan was not offering Him a shortcut to God's kingdom. He was offering Him a choice between Satan's kingdom and God's kingdom. There are no shortcuts. Jesus could not have the crown without the cross. So again, reaching back to Deuteronomy, Jesus quoted, "YOU SHALL WORSHIP THE LORD YOUR GOD, AND SERVE HIM ONLY" (Deut 6:13). True worship cannot be a one-time experience. True worship is followed by a life of service.

The Principle

Choose to serve God in your life. Beware of the temptation to have all that this world offers as well as all that God offers. It often has been said, "When it is too good to be true, it is." Jesus said two chapters later in Matthew 6, "You cannot serve God and wealth" (6:24). There are no shortcuts to God's will and way. He calls us to a life of worship and service. To worship means to fall down before Him and show Him respect, honor, and reverence. We cannot worship God on Sunday and live for the world the rest of the week. That is a misrepresentation. But that is what Satan was suggesting, and many people have been deceived by this very offer. Jesus reminds us that true worship is followed by a life of service to God, and He urges us, "Seek first His kingdom and His righteousness, and all these things will be added to you" (Matt. 6:33).

Conclusion

With this last temptation Jesus ordered Satan to leave. These temptations proved the complete faithfulness and worthiness of Jesus Christ to be our Savior. As we face our own temptations, we can rest in the truth that we have a faithful high priest who understands our struggles and prays for us in the victory He has already won: "For we do not have a high priest who cannot sympathize with our weaknesses, but One who has been tempted in all things as *we are, yet* without sin" (Heb. 4:15).

Temptation in itself is not wrong. The struggle, the challenge, or the process of temptation is a part of our spiritual conflict. But in Jesus Christ God transforms Satan's temptations into a demonstration of His grace in our lives. How does He do that? He does it as we face these temptations in the same way Jesus faced temptation. And the key to every response of Jesus was the Word of God. God's truth must be a part of our thinking so that we know where to go in time of temptation. As we prayerfully apply the Word of God and choose God over the passing pleasures of this world, we will experience a growing relationship with Jesus Christ.

What is your temptation or trial this day? Are you tempted to substitute the world's ways for God's way? Refuse to meet that legitimate need in a wrong way. Are you tempted to test God, to demand that God do this or that for you? Trust Him rather than test Him. Are you tempted to take a shortcut in God's purpose for your life? Choose to worship and serve God rather than give your life to another purpose.

Prophecies of Christ

TOM TRIGGS

PROPHECY	OLD TESTAMENT	NEW TESTAMENT
Christ's preexistence	Micah 5:2	John 1:1, 14
All nations blessed by Abraham's seed	Genesis 12:3	Matthew 8:5-10
Lamb provided by God as an Offering	Genesis 22:2	John 1:29
From Tribe of Judah	Genesis 49:10	Luke 3:33
Heir to the throne of David	Isaiah 9:7	Luke 1:32-33
Called "The mighty God, The Everlasting Father"	Isaiah 9:6	Matthew 1:23
Born in Bethlehem	Micah 5:2	Matthew 2:1
Born of a virgin	Isaiah 7:14	Matthew 1:18
His name called Immanuel, "God with us"	Isaiah 7:14	Matthew 1:23
Declared to be the Son of God	Psalm 2:7	Matthew 3:17
Messenger sent before Him in spirit of Elijah	Malachi 4:5-6	Luke 1:17

Preceded by a messenger	Malachi 3:1	Matthew 11:7-11
Messenger crying, "Make ready the way of the Lord"	Isaiah 40:3	Matthew 3:3
Would be a prophet of the children of Israel	Deuteronomy 18:15	Matthew 2:15
Called out of Egypt	Hosea 11:1	Matthew 2:15
Slaughter of the children	Jeremiah 31:15	Matthew 2:18
Would be a Nazarene	Judges 13:5; Amos 2:11	Matthew 2:23
Would bring light to Zebulon, Naphtali, Galiee	Isaiah 9:1-2	Matthew 4:15
Presented with Gifts	Psalm 72:10	Matthew 2:1, 11
Rejected by His own	Isaiah 53:3	Matthew 21:42; Mark 8:31; 12:10; Luke 9:22; 17:25
He is the stone the builders rejected, which became the headstone	Psalm 118:22-23; Isaiah 28:16	Matthew 21:42; 1 Peter 2:7
A stone of stumbling to Israel	Isaiah 8:14-15	1 Peter 2:8
Entered Jerusalem as a king riding on an ass	Zechariah 9:9	Matthew 21:5

Betrayed by a friend	Psalm 41:9	John 13:21
Sold for 30 pieces of silver	Zechariah 11:12	Matthew 26:15; Luke 22:5
30 pieces of silver for the potter's field	Zechariah 11:12	Matthew 27:9-10
The 30 pieces of silver thrown in the temple	Zechariah 11:13	Matthew 27:5
Forsaken by his disciples	Zechariah 13:7	Matthew 26:56
Accused by false witnesses	Psalm 35:11	Matthew 26:60
Silent to accusations	Isaiah 53:7	Matthew 27:14
Healed blind, deaf, lame, dumb	Isaiah 29:18; 35:5-6	Matthew 11:5
Preached to the afflicted	Isaiah 61:1	Matthew 11:5

3

A Miracle of Forgiveness

(Mark 2:1-12)

JOHN FRENCH

Let's begin by taking a quick tour of Mark's Gospel. Mark emphasizes the work, the activity, and the miracles of Jesus. He does not spend a lot of time on the teaching of Jesus or upon His personal background. So the theme of Mark's presentation is ministry—the ministry of God's Servant, God's Messiah.

We see Jesus' ministry in three main areas. The first is His ministry in and to society. Here Jesus presents Himself as the coming Messiah. In the second major section of Mark, Jesus instructs and teaches His disciples. The largest section of the book presents Jesus' ministry leading up to the cross. At the beginning and end, there are short sections introducing and concluding Jesus' ministry.

MARK: THE MINISTRY OF JESUS, THE MESSIAH

INTRO	*SOCIETY*	*DISCIPLES*	*CROSS*	*CONCLU-SION*
1:1-13	*1:14–3:6*	*3:7–10:52*	*11:1–16:14*	*16:15-20*

Chapter 2 is the heart of Jesus' ministry to society. In the five incidents recorded in this chapter, Jesus challenges the prevailing ideas of His day. God's truth always does that. If you talk about family values, sexual standards, true happiness, materialism, personal rights, the authority of the Bible, or the person of Christ, you will always find some resistance, even from the religious community. God's truth requires us to rethink the basic areas of our lives.

This miracle of forgiveness in Mark 2:1-12 reveals the true identity of Jesus and why Jesus is sufficient to meet our every need. Forgiveness comes through faith in the person of Christ.

The Faith of Five Men (Mark 2:1-5)

> *1 When He had come back to Capernaum several days afterward, it was heard that He was at home. 2 And many were gathered together, so that there was no longer room, not even near the door; and He was speaking the word to them. 3 And they came, bringing to Him a paralytic, carried by four men. 4 Being unable to get to Him because of the crowd, they removed the roof above Him; and when they had dug an opening, they let down the pallet on which the paralytic was lying. 5 And Jesus seeing their faith said to the paralytic, "Son, your sins are forgiven."*

Verse 5 says that Jesus saw "their faith." Specifically, he saw the faith of the paralyzed man and the four men who brought him to see the Lord. Notice the three qualities of these men's faith.

Active Faith

These four friends carried the news to their paralyzed friend that Jesus had returned to Capernaum. From what they had seen and heard, they knew Jesus could provide help for their friend when no one else could. They not only thought about it and talked about it and perhaps prayed about it, but they also acted upon the knowledge that Jesus was there to help. They loaded their friend onto a pallet and carried him to see Jesus.

Persistent Faith

The closer they came to the home where Jesus was, the more people clogged the streets. It took hard work to jostle the awkward mat through the crowds. When they arrived, they discovered that it was impossible to get anywhere close to Jesus because of the throng that had gathered to hear His teaching. They could have said, "There are too many people." "We will come back another day." "It must not be God's will." "We don't want to stand in line all day." "It will take too much time." There is a danger in trusting circumstances for discerning God's will. Satan will always put obstacles in the way. We will always experience resistance to our faith. There are always circumstantial reasons why a ministry shouldn't or couldn't be done.

But these men had a persistent faith. They believed there was no other way for their friend to be healed apart from meeting Jesus. They were willing and resourceful to keep at it until they had made that possible.

Many homes of that day were flat-roofed. The roof would be constructed of beams laid across the walls. Branches would serve as supporting cross pieces, topped with a layer of brush, dirt, clay, or some mixture of several of these. The men made their way to the roof of the house, probably by means of an outside stairway, and pulled back or dug through this top layer so that they could create space between the main supporting beams and lower the stretcher into the presence of Jesus.

Successful Faith

Jesus did not criticize these men for their unorthodox way of getting the job done. He recognized the genuineness of their faith by responding to meet the need. He saw that at least five men in the crowd were concerned not only with physical needs but also with spiritual needs. They were coming with the hope that this teacher who could heal the body would also heal the heart. That is the faith Jesus saw, and that is why He responded with both healing and forgiveness. "*Seeing* their faith," he said, "Son, your sins are forgiven."

Our Faith

The faith we see here emphasizes our absolute trust in the sufficiency of Christ to meet our needs. We look for no other alternatives. I believe many times we struggle or fail in the Christian life because we are looking for our options. These men had no Plan B. It was Christ or nothing. We need that kind of tenacity in our faith.

One of my favorite illustrations about trust is the man who went walking along a narrow path in the mountains. Not paying much attention to where he was going, he suddenly slipped over the edge of the cliff. As he fell, he grabbed a branch growing from the side of the cliff. Realizing that he couldn't hang on for long, he called for help.

Man: Is anybody up there?

Voice: Yes, I'm here!

Man: Who's that?

Voice: The Lord.

Man: Lord, help me!

Voice: Do you trust me?

Man: I trust you completely, Lord.

Voice: Good. Let go of the branch.

Man: What?

Voice: I said, "Let go of the branch."

Man (after a long pause): Is anybody else up there?[1]

For what do you need to trust God today? As you exercise an active and persistent faith, you will have a successful faith. This is true because of who Jesus is.

---

[1] Michael Green, ed., *Illustrations for Biblical Preaching* (Grand Rapids: Baker, 1989), 138.

The Person of Jesus (Mark 2:6-12)

> [6] *But some of the scribes were sitting there and reasoning in their hearts,* [7] *"Why does this man speak that way? He is blaspheming; who can forgive sins but God alone?"* [8] *Immediately Jesus, aware in His spirit that they were reasoning that way within themselves, said to them, "Why are you reasoning about these things in your hearts?* [9] *"Which is easier, to say to the paralytic, 'Your sins are forgiven'; or to say, 'Get up, and pick up your pallet and walk'?* [10] *"But so that you may know that the Son of Man has authority on earth to forgive sins"—He said to the paralytic,* [11] *"I say to you, get up, pick up your pallet and go home."* [12] *And he got up and immediately picked up the pallet and went out in the sight of everyone, so that they were all amazed and were glorifying God, saying, "We have never seen anything like this."*

Importance

The death and resurrection of Jesus are central events in the life of Christ. But those events have meaning because of who He is. Earlier in Mark, His miracles demonstrate the divine authority of Jesus. The miracle we see here demonstrates His complete equality with God, for we find Jesus doing what only God can do.

Problem

The scribes (teachers of the law) came up out of their chairs when they heard Jesus say, "Your sins are forgiven." They were still thinking to themselves, but they were all thinking the same thing: "He can't say that. He is blaspheming, for only God can forgive sins." Were they right? Speaking of the Lord (Yahweh), Psalm 130:4 says, "But there is forgiveness with You, that You may be feared." In Isaiah 43:25, the LORD (the Redeemer, the Holy One of Israel) promises, "I, even I, am the one who wipes out your transgressions for My own sake, and I will not remember your sins." Jesus' opponents knew that only God could forgive sins.

To blaspheme means to speak evil of someone. We can blaspheme another person, and we blaspheme God any time we misuse his name. Exodus 20:7 says, "You shall not misuse the name of the LORD your God, for the LORD will not hold anyone guiltless who misuses his name" (NIV). When David Koresh proclaimed himself a messiah, or when a TV evangelist swindles millions out of his viewers, or when any Christian sleeps around or exploits his or her employees, that is blasphemy against God because it misuses and misrepresents the name of God. That is what the scribes and Pharisees[2] thought was happening here. Of course, if it were true, it would be a most serious matter.

Proof

Jesus understood the debate raging in their minds, and so He took the challenge to them. "Which is easier, to say to the paralytic, 'Your sins are forgiven'; or to say 'Get up, and pick up your pallet and walk'?" The question is which of these two statements is easier to *say*. Forgiveness is a spiritual matter. It cannot be proved or disproved. But people will immediately know whether you have healed a person or not. Both require supernatural power to do. The ability to do the one (physically heal) would confirm Jesus' authority and ability to do the other (forgive). Jesus told the man to take up his mat and go home. That is exactly what the man did in full view of everyone there, once again showing the unquestionable reality of Jesus' power.

Response

"If only God can forgive sins eternally and if He, Jesus, had just done that, then Jesus must be God."[3] That was the conclusion Jesus

---

[2] The parallel passages in Matthew 9:1-8 and Luke 5:17-26 reveal that Pharisees were also present. In the New Testament, the Pharisaic party of the Jews, whose legalistic approach to the Mosaic law as well as their own man-made laws led them to consistently oppose Jesus, are often mentioned together with the scribes, many of whom may have been Pharisees as well.

[3] Charles Ryrie, *The Miracles of Our Lord* (Nashville: Nelson, 1984), 51.

was looking for. Ultimately, Jesus wants our trust because we believe He is the Son of God.

The response of the people was similar to what we have seen before. They were amazed. Literally, the word means "beside themselves" or "out of their minds." But it appears they still were amazed with what He was doing, not so much with who He was. The Pharisees were definitely not impressed, however. They had heard words they considered blasphemy, and they saw a teacher growing in power and influence. Jesus continued to challenge their traditions so that in Mark 3:6 we read, "The Pharisees went out and immediately *began* conspiring with the Herodians against Him, *as to how they might destroy Him.*" They had made their choice.

Conclusion

Each of us must make a decision concerning the claims of Christ. But what choices do we have concerning Christ?[4]

First, consider the possibility that Jesus' claim to be God was false. If it were, then we have two and only two alternatives: He either knew His claim was false, or He didn't. If, when Jesus made this claim, He knew He was not God, then He was lying. But if He was a liar, then He was also a hypocrite, because He told others to be honest whatever the cost, while He Himself was living a lie. He would also be a fool because it was His claim of being God that led to His crucifixion.

If it is inconceivable that Jesus was a liar, then could He not actually have *thought* Himself to be God but been mistaken? After all, it is possible to be both sincere and wrong. But we must remember that someone who thinks he is God, especially in a culture that is fiercely monotheistic, and then tells others that their eternal destinies depend upon their believing in him is indulging in no small fantasy. These would be the thoughts of a lunatic. But could an in-

---

[4] These thoughts come from the writings of C. S. Lewis and have been popularized by Josh McDowell. See chapter 2, "Lord, Liar, or Lunatic?" in Josh McDowell, *More Than a Carpenter* (Wheaton: Tyndale, 1977), 25-35.

sane man have delivered the Sermon on the Mount, related the warmth of the parables, or tenderly healed the sick?

The whole picture of Jesus' teachings and ministry make it untenable to believe that He was either a liar or a lunatic. Therefore, His claims must be true. He is Lord and God, and there are only two options available to us: we can accept Him as Savior and Lord, or we can reject Him and suffer the consequences of our decision.

The scribes and Pharisees chose to reject the claims of Christ. The paralyzed man and his friends chose faith in the person of Christ and received the miracle of forgiveness. You, too, can make this Christ the Lord of your life. The Bible says, "Believe in the Lord Jesus, and you will be saved" (Acts 16:31).

Jewish Religious Parties Mentioned in the Gospels

JARL K. WAGGONER

	Pharisees	Sadducees
Principal Beliefs	[1]Strict adherence to law [2]Oral traditions equated with OT law [3]Believed in resurrection of body and life after death [4]Separated ones who considered themselves righteous and others sinners	[1]Considered law of Moses as final authority, even above rest of OT [2]Rationalists who denied existence of angels, resurrection of body, and future life [3]Willing to adapt to political and cultural changes
Gospel References	Matt. 3:7; 5:20; 12:14; 23:13, 15, 23, 25, 27, 29; Mark 7:3, 5; Luke 11:42-43; 12:1; John 7:32; 18:3; etc.	Matt. 3:7; 16:6; 22:23, 34; Mark 16:12; etc.
Influence	Largest religious party	Party that dominated the Sanhedrin
Associated Groups	*Scribes* (Legal Scholars – Most were Pharisees) *Zealots* (Primarily political— Advocated overthrow of Roman rule)	*Scribes* (Legal Scholars – Some were Sadducees) *Herodians* (Primarily political— Supported Herodian rulers and Romans)

4

Power Play

(Mark 4:35-5:43)

LEE COMPSON

Have you ever had a stretch of really good "luck," when incredible things kept happening to you? I had one of those stretches in high school. We were at Word of Life camp in upstate New York and had arrived a few days after some severe storms had knocked out power and damaged some of the property.

It was fine for the first few hours and the first day. But by the second day, I remember feeling frustrated at the inconveniences and saying, "Man, I wish the lights would come on." Literally, the instant I said that, the lights came on.

Later that same summer at home, it had been raining, and I said, "Man, I wish it would quit raining." Very soon after that, the rain completely stopped.

My good fortune continued the next summer when I discovered a new brand of soda pop named Surge. It was a delicious, Mountain Dew-type drink, and at the time it was carrying a promotion under the cap where you could win a free Surge. I had a streak in which five out of six bottles I bought within a couple weeks rewarded me a free one.

If I didn't know any better, I might have thought I had acquired special powers with all these cool coincidences that were happening to me.

While we can always dream of having that kind of real power, we know no one can control the weather or forecast the future—no one but Jesus, that is. Being God allowed Him on special occasions to display His divine power and authority in helping people who were in need. The Gospels record many of these encounters, and the book of Mark contains a concentrated section in 4:35–5:43.

Here there are three stories recorded back to back to back that teach us how *Jesus controls the uncontrollable and fixes what's beyond repair.*

This section of the Gospels can be especially comforting to us today, because while we may enjoy stretches of "good luck" and nice coincidences, eventually life will get hard.

"When life gives you lemons, make lemonade." It's a well-worn cliché that people often use as inspiration. But this cliché ignores the reality that it is impossible to make good lemonade from rotten, sour, worm-infested lemons. And sometimes life's lemons—the trials of life—are just that bad. A cliché like that is just an empty phrase when life is spinning out of control and situations seem hopelessly broken.

Thankfully we don't have to handle life's trials on our own. We have a Savior in Jesus who controls the uncontrollable and can fix what's beyond repair.

Jesus' Power *Delivers* Us from Our Fear (Mark 4:35-41)

> [35] On that day, when evening came, He said to them, "Let us go over to the other side." [36] Leaving the crowd, they took Him along with them in the boat, just as He was; and other boats were with Him. [37] And there arose a fierce gale of wind, and the waves were breaking over the boat so much that the boat was already filling up. [38] Jesus Himself was in the stern, asleep on the cushion; and they woke Him and said to Him, "Teacher, do You not care that we are perishing?" [39] And He got up and rebuked the wind and said to the sea, "Hush, be still." And the wind died down and it became perfectly calm. [40] And He said to them, "Why are you afraid? Do you still have no faith?" [41] They became very much afraid and said to one another, "Who then is this, that even the wind and the sea obey Him?"

Jesus and His disciples found themselves in a seemingly uncontrollable situation, as a rough storm came up as they sailed across the Sea of Galilee. The fact that many of these disciples were veteran fishermen who were experienced in navigating normal storms highlights the severity of the weather and the sense of danger and tension in this event. If these veteran fishermen were scared of the weather, it must have been pretty bad.

But this extreme storm was no match for the power of Jesus. This miracle demonstrates how Jesus' power delivers us from our fears.

Our Fears Reveal Our Lack of Faith (vv. 35-40)

This is a pretty famous miracle of Jesus—so famous that we in our own Christian-ese language often talk about Jesus "calming the storms of our life." While that may be a clichéd way to apply this story to our lives, this miracle can force us to look in the mirror at our own doubts and fears and how *our fears reveal our lack of faith*.

The disciples had seen Jesus' power previously, and they should have known they would be safe with Jesus.[1] But they panicked in the storm (v. 38), and Jesus admonished them for their lack of faith after He miraculously calmed the storm (v. 40).[2] The trials of life that affect us also may reveal our lack of faith and trust in our God. We may focus too much on the circumstances and not enough on our all-powerful God.

Jesus Possesses Unlimited Power—Even over Nature (v. 39)

While some are quick to make a symbol out of this story, in its essence, this miracle revolves around an intense patch of bad weather. Think about recent hurricanes—Katrina, Sandy, Irene— and the devastation they left in their wake. As human beings, we can create the illusion of safety, security, and protection. But

---

[1] See Mark 2:1-12 and 3:7-12 as two such examples.

[2] "So lack of faith makes disciples *deiloi,* unable to respond to a crisis with confidence in God ... which is the mark of a true disciple" (R. T. France, *The Gospel of Mark: A Commentary on the Greek Text* (Grand Rapids: Eerdmans, 2002), 225.

storms like those are horrific reminders of our limited power and control.

Jesus stands in stark contrast to that reality. He simply spoke, and the storm was immediately gone. The danger was over, and the sea was calm. That is incredible power and authority. While our fear might get the best of us and reveal that we are not truly trusting in the Lord for the help we need, this miracle offers us hope. It assures us we serve a Savior who is all-powerful and worthy of our faith.

Jesus' Power Should Inspire Awe (v. 41)

The disciples' response shows how limited their view of Christ had been. While some translations use the term "awe" in verse 41, the term is a little more nuanced than that simple translation. The NASB more accurately translates *phobos megas* as "very much afraid." This is not a cowardly fear (*deilos*), as in verse 40, but "the appropriate response of humans faced with ... divine power or glory."[3]

God's power should inspire fearful awe in us as well. Even the most well-intentioned Christian will "put God in a box" from time to time, limiting Him and His abilities in their own minds. When we properly focus on who God is and what He is capable of, awe is a perfectly fitting response.

We can take heart, too, in that these were Jesus' closest companions and they still had room to grow. They didn't fully get who Jesus is—in fact, they even asked, "Who then is this?"

Hopefully as we grow in our faith, we will be able to cast our cares on Christ in a deeper and more comprehensive way. Whatever your current fears are, take heart that Jesus' power delivers us from our fear.

Jesus' Power *Frees* Us from Evil (Mark 5:1-20)

> [1]*They came to the other side of the sea, into the country of the Gerasenes.* [2] *When He got out of the boat, immediately a man from the tombs with an un-*

---

[3] Ibid.

clean spirit met Him, [3] *and he had his dwelling among the tombs. And no one was able to bind him anymore, even with a chain;* [4] *because he had often been bound with shackles and chains, and the chains had been torn apart by him and the shackles broken in pieces, and no one was strong enough to subdue him.* [5] *Constantly, night and day, he was screaming among the tombs and in the mountains, and gashing himself with stones.* [6] *Seeing Jesus from a distance, he ran up and bowed down before Him;* [7] *and shouting with a loud voice, he said, "What business do we have with each other, Jesus, Son of the Most High God? I implore You by God, do not torment me!"* [8] *For He had been saying to him, "Come out of the man, you unclean spirit!"* [9] *And He was asking him, "What is your name?" And he said to Him, "My name is Legion; for we are many."* [10] *And he began to implore Him earnestly not to send them out of the country.* [11] *Now there was a large herd of swine feeding nearby on the mountain.* [12] *The demons implored Him, saying, "Send us into the swine so that we may enter them."* [13] *Jesus gave them permission. And coming out, the unclean spirits entered the swine; and the heard rushed down the steep bank into the sea, about two thousand of them; and they were drowned in the sea.*

[14] *Their herdsmen ran away and reported it in the city and in the country. And the people came to see what it was that had happened.* [15] *They came to Jesus and observed the man who had been demon-possessed sitting down, clothed and in his right mind, the very man who had had the "legion"; and they became frightened.* [16] *Those who had seen it described to them how it had happened to the demon-possessed man, and all about the swine.* [17] *And they began to implore Him to leave their region.* [18] *As He was get-*

ting into the boat, the man who had been demon-possessed was imploring Him that he might ac-company Him. [19] And He did not let him, but He said to him, "Go home to your people and report to them what great things the Lord has done for you, and how He had mercy on you." [20] And he went away and began to proclaim in Decapolis what great things Jesus had done for him; and everyone was amazed.

Jesus and His disciples finished their journey and ended up on the eastern side of the Sea of Galilee, in Gentile territory. Immediately upon their arrival, they were confronted with another scary and potentially out-of-control situation.

Evil Spirits Recognize and Submit to Jesus' Power (vv. 1-13)

Hollywood loves to make scary movies because apparently people in our society enjoy being freaked out and having nightmares when they sleep. Just in the past several years, there has been an increase in demon-possession and exorcism movies made by big Hollywood studios: *The Devil Inside, The Last Exorcism, The Rite, Constantine, The Exorcism of Emily Rose, Paranormal Activity.* I don't watch those and would strongly advise you to avoid them too. But the fact that they are made proves that people are fascinated by the supernatural world and the evil forces at work. While we may want to avoid those movies, we should not ignore the fact that demons and demon possessions are real.

Confronted with this reality in the form of this out-of-control, demon-possessed man, Jesus displayed His power over evil.

In the previous story, the disciples had wondered, "Who is this?" Ironically, it is the demons who provide the answer. Jesus is the "Son of the Most High God" (v. 7). He is divine and posed a threat to the demons occupying this man just by His presence. And they have to submit to Jesus when He commands them to leave the man's body (vv. 8-13). Just as the violent storm obeyed Christ, *evil spirits must recognize and submit to Jesus' power.*

A Changed Life Is an Effective Witness to Jesus' Power (vv. 14-20)

Our attention is quickly drawn to the fact that the demons were sent into the pigs and they then drown (v. 13). Certainly that shows the destructive power of the evil forces and proves they have to obey Jesus. But don't miss the contrast between this wild, crazy person who approached Jesus (vv. 2-5) and the calm and serene person who remained after the demons left (v. 15). This is a stark example of *how a changed life is an effective witness to Jesus' power.*

Word quickly spread about what Jesus had done (v. 14). The people from this region, mostly Gentiles, responded out of fear. It seems Jesus had disrupted their "normal" lives, and they asked Him to leave (v. 17). They were likely driven by pagan superstition or a strong concern about the loss of property that the local herdsmen experienced.

While Jesus acquiesced to their request, He didn't leave them alone to fend for themselves. Mark makes it clear in verses 18-20 that this formerly demon-possessed man was given a mission by Jesus to share with others the work God had done in his life. His life had been dramatically changed by God, and Jesus left him in this Gentile region to be a witness to His power.

Jesus delivers us from our fear, and Jesus' power frees us from evil. Whatever sins we personally struggle with, Jesus' power offers us freedom. God offers us the power we need to be free from sin and to be free for our mission. Like this man, we too are called to be a witness to those family, friends, and neighbors around us. God has changed us and continues to change us. That life-changing power will help us be effective witnesses for Christ.

Jesus' Power *Conquers* Our Suffering (Mark 5:21-43)

> [21] *When Jesus had crossed over again in the boat to the other side, a large crowd gathered around Him; and so He stayed by the seashore.* [22] *One of the synagogue officials named Jairus came up, and on seeing Him, fell at His feet* [23] *and implored Him earnestly,*

saying, "My little daughter is at the point of death; please come and lay Your hands on her, so that she will get well and live." [24] And He went off with him; and a large crowd was following Him and pressing in on Him.

[25] A woman who had had a hemorrhage for twelve years, [26] and had endured much at the hands of many physicians, and had spent all that she had and was not helped at all, but rather had grown worse— [27] after hearing about Jesus, she came up in the crowd behind Him and touched His cloak. [28] For she thought, "If I just touch His garments, I will get well." [29] Immediately the flow of her blood was dried up; and she felt in her body that she was healed of her affliction. [30] Immediately Jesus, perceiving in Himself that the power proceeding from Him had gone forth, turned around in the crowd and said, "Who touched My garments?" [31] And His disciples said to Him, "You see the crowd pressing in on You, and You say, 'Who touched Me?'" [32] And He looked around to see the woman who had done this. [33] But the woman fearing and trembling, aware of what had happened to her, came and fell down before Him and told Him the whole truth. [34] And He said to her, "Daughter, your faith has made you well; go in peace and be healed of your affliction."

[35] While He was still speaking, they came from the house of the synagogue official, saying, "Your daughter has died; why trouble the Teacher anymore?" [36] But Jesus, overhearing what was being spoken, said to the synagogue official, "Do not be afraid any longer, only believe." [37] And He allowed no one to accompany Him, except Peter and James and John the brother of James. [38] They came to the house of the synagogue official; and He saw a commotion, and

people loudly weeping and wailing. [39] *And entering in, He said to them, "Why make a commotion and weep? The child has not died, but is asleep."* [40] *They began laughing at Him. But putting them all out, He took along the child's father and mother and His own companions, and entered the room where the child was.* [41] *Taking the child by the hand, He said to her, "Talitha kum!" (which translated means, "Little girl, I say to you, get up!").* [42] *Immediately the girl got up and began to walk, for she was twelve years old. And immediately they were completely astounded.* [43] *And He gave them strict orders that no one should know about this, and He said that something should be given her to eat.*

The third and final miracle story within this passage actually develops into two separate miracle accounts. One involves a serious sickness; the other, death.

Jesus Can Help Anyone (vv. 21-25a)

The first thing to notice as this scene unfolds is the contrast between the two individuals who came seeking Jesus' help. One was a man of great importance (a synagogue official) and the other a woman of no importance. *Jesus can help anyone.* Our social status does not matter. The size of our bank account does not matter. Our reputation does not matter. Jesus reached out to a prominent religious official, as well as an anonymous woman who was a social outcast. Interestingly enough, Jesus interrupted His work on behalf of the man of significant social status to help the woman who was of no social importance.

Jesus Can Help Anyone with Anything (vv. 25b-27, 35-43)

Not only can Jesus help anyone, but *He can help anyone with anything.* These two individuals were dealing with different yet extremely significant problems. The woman was experiencing a horrible illness that was causing her to suffer, not just physically, but socially and spiritually as well. Ponder the position this disease had put her in.

- No doctor could help her.
- She had run out of money due to paying doctors who had been unable to help her.
- Her condition, which she had battled for twelve years, was actually worsening.
- Because of her condition, she was "unclean" and could not go to the temple to worship God (cf. Lev. 15:19-27).
- She may have been divorced because she could not have children.[4]

This woman was the most outcast person one could find, given the culture and context of the story. But Jesus helped her with her seemingly insurmountable problem.

Jesus continued to display His power over suffering when He arrived at Jairus's home. All seemed lost when the news of his daughter's death reached Jairus (v. 35). But Jesus stepped in and miraculously raised the girl back to life. Homer Kent Jr. comments,

> One can visualize how this twelve-year-old girl must have darted from one parent to the other when she was restored. The great astonishment of the witnesses needs no comment. If anything, it is an understatement.[5]

Jesus Cares Less about Proper Procedure than Proper Faith (vv. 28-43)

As the woman initially approached Jesus, we are told she was thinking, "If I just touch His garments, I will get well" (v. 28). It is likely this reflected a superstitious belief; but when Jesus addressed

---

[4] "Since she appears alone in public and draws on her own resources to pay the physicians (vs. 26), [she] may also have been 'dismissed' or divorced" (John R. Donahue and Daniel J. Harrington, *The Gospel of Mark* (Collegeville, MN: Liturgical Press, 2002), 180.

[5] Homer A. Kent Jr., *Mark: The Beginning of the Gospel of Jesus Christ* (Winona Lake, IN: BMH, 2005), 77.

her, He made it clear that she was healed because of her faith in Him (v. 34).[6] Her theology may not have been 100 percent correct, but her faith was in the right place. This part of the story, combined with the fact that He allowed an unclean woman to touch him and intentionally touched a dead girl's body Himself (v. 41), leads us to realize that *Jesus cared less about proper procedure and more about proper faith.*

People in need do not have to have all their "ducks in a row" or have everything figured out. They just need to turn to Christ. This is true of the unsaved, as well as those of us who are saved. Whether our need is salvation or related to the sufferings of this life, the solution is found by placing our faith and trust in Jesus.

Jesus' power conquers, not just incurable sickness, but also death—spiritual and physical death. Jesus heals and brings life. His power conquers our suffering. Sickness and death are horrible and unavoidable consequences of sin, but Jesus' power and ultimately His death give us victory over those things.

Conclusion

When I was in college, several of my friends loved to play a game called "Would You Rather?" It's a game designed to gross each other out and imagine what sort of pain tolerance you would have in made-up scenarios.

For example, someone might ask: "Would you rather get punched in the face or have your foot run over by a dump truck?"

Or a player might offer this pleasant setup: "Would you rather have your knee hit with a sledge hammer or your pinky cut off with a saw?"

I was always looking for a third option. Thankfully, there's very little chance of having to actually make those choices. But sometimes we are confronted with situations that are very problematic and cannot be avoided. Sometimes we are forced to deal with uncontrollable and very scary situations. Sometimes we find our-

---

[6] Ibid., 74.

selves struggling with sin and evil in a very serious sense. At other times we must deal with suffering, whether sickness or death.

This group of miracles teaches us how Jesus is able to control the uncontrollable and fix what's beyond repair. We have an all-powerful and all-loving Savior. He will deliver us from our fears. He will free us from evil. He will conquer our suffering. Whatever circumstances may confronted us, we can have confidence in the power of Christ to control what's uncontrollable and fix what's broken beyond repair.

5

Jesus' First Lesson on Prayer

(Matthew 5:43-48)

JARL K. WAGGONER

When Andrew Murray wrote his classic, *With Christ in the School of Prayer,* he began his study with Luke 11:1: "Lord, teach us to pray." R. A. Torrey's book, *How to Pray,* begins with a chapter on the importance of prayer. While these are good places to start when taking up the great subject of prayer, Jesus began His instruction on prayer in a very different place.

While it is certainly wise—if not necessary—to systematize biblical teaching in order to understand the full range of divine truth in all its relationships, Jesus' teaching was not presented in what we think of as a "systematic" form—point I, point IA, point IB, and so on. Rather, He taught His disciples and others in the context of life and ministry together as the occasion warranted, and so it was with His teaching on prayer.

Jesus' first recorded instruction on prayer, both biblically and chronologically, is found in the Sermon on the Mount. That first lesson does not deal with the nature or definition of prayer, the importance of prayer, how to pray, or when to pray. Instead, His first instruction concerning prayer is this: *Pray for your enemies.* On the face of it, this is almost shocking! Surely this should be the *last* lesson on prayer. Only graduates of the Lord's school of prayer should be able to pray for their enemies!

One of the keys to understanding Jesus' teaching on prayer here, as well as much of the Sermon on the Mount, is His statement in Matthew 5:20: "Unless your righteousness surpasses that of the scribes and Pharisees, you will not enter the kingdom of heaven." Jesus then went on to describe a righteousness that exceeds that of the scribes and Pharisees.[1] The righteousness of those smug religious elitists was merely outward; it did not touch and transform the heart. The righteousness of true kingdom citizens is based on the imputed righteousness of Christ that comes through faith in Him. It flows from a transformed heart and is revealed in a godly life that looks beyond mere outward standards to a person's thoughts and motivations.

The Contrast (Matt. 5:43)

> [43] *"You have heard that it was said, 'YOU SHALL LOVE YOUR NEIGHBOR and hate your enemy.'*

Before instructing His disciples, Jesus gave a contrasting view: that of the scribes and Pharisees. Though they are not named in this verse, it is clear from Jesus' repeated statement—beginning in verse 21—that His hearers had "heard it said," that what follows this statement in each instance is the teaching of the scribes and Pharisees (v. 20). Here He said what people commonly heard from these religious leaders was, "You shall love your neighbor and hate your enemy."

Indeed, God had commanded love for one's neighbors in Leviticus 19:18, and Jesus upheld this as the "second" greatest commandment (Matt. 22:36-40). However, nowhere in Scripture is there a command to hate one's enemies. In fact, Leviticus 19:18 emphasizes "*love* over against *vengeance.*"[2] Yet, the scribes and

---

[1] The Pharisees were legalists. They held a very strict interpretation of the Mosaic law, but they also added to that law their own rules, which were counted as important as God's. While there were exceptions, Jesus strongly denounced the Pharisees as a whole for their self-righteous attitudes that stressed outward observances while ignoring the inward attitudes. The scribes are frequently mentioned along with the Pharisees. They were legal scholars who also concerned themselves with minutiae of the law at the expense of humility, compassion, justice, and other godly virtues. Many, if not most, of the scribes also belonged to the Pharisaic party. Jesus' most scathing comments are reserved for the scribes and Pharisees (cf. Matt. 23).

[2] William Hendriksen, *The Gospel of Matthew,* New Testament Commentary (Grand Rapids: Baker, 1973), 312.

Pharisees assumed that a command to love one's neighbors implicitly authorized hatred of one's enemies, and apparently this was a popular interpretation.[3] Beyond this, though, hatred of one's enemies is the way of the world. It is natural (for fallen man) and easy.

The Instruction (Matt. 5:44)

[44] *"But I say to you, love your enemies and pray for those who persecute you,*

Jesus' instruction to His disciples stood in sharp contrast to the commonly held belief that one should hate his or her enemies. Jesus said, "Love your enemies and pray for those who persecute you." Such a statement was shocking, not only because it contrasted with the teaching of the scribes and Pharisees, but also because it was something no one taught. Jesus' teaching here follows shortly after His choosing of the Twelve (cf. Matt. 4:18-22). So, again, we might well have thought He would have started with something a little more basic and a little less shocking.[4]

Jesus' statement is a twofold command: to love and to pray. There is clear parallelism in the command. The enemies we are to love are the persecutors we are to pray for. Thus, to love them *is* to pray for them. Love is the subject, but we show love for them by praying for them. The Greek word for "enemies" *(echthros)* refers to hateful people—those who hate us. Persecutors, literally, are those who pursue us. It is not required that we be fond of these people or approve of their actions in order to love them. Christlike love is not a feeling but a commitment to doing what is beneficial for another person, and prayer is certainly beneficial.

---

[3] Homer A. Kent Jr. ("Matthew" in *Wycliffe Bible Commentary,* ed. Charles F. Pfeiffer and Everett F. Harrison [Chicago: Moody, 1962], 939) points out that the Qumran Manual of Discipline, found among the Dead Sea Scrolls, contains a similar statement.

[4] Note: KJV and NKJV include other words here taken from Luke 6:27-28. NASB omits these words from Matthew 5:43 on the basis of manuscript evidence.

We should note here, too, that the true measure of our love for people—especially our enemies—is not outward, public conformity to a certain standard. Of course, our public actions toward all people should be above reproach, but the Lord measures our love for people by our private prayers on their behalf.

Praying for our enemies does not mean praying for deliverance from them or praying for their destruction, though such prayer may at times be legitimate, as the Psalms demonstrate. "For" (*huper*) means to pray in their behalf—intercede for them. Such prayers are also for our benefit in that this is "the best way to prevent a bitter spirit from getting a grip on us."[5] Obeying this command may not require emotion, but it will produce it.

This is the essence of Christlike love: praying for our enemies. We see this exemplified in our Lord's prayer for those who crucified Him (Luke 23:34) and in Stephen's dying prayer for his persecutors (Acts 7:60).

The Motivation (Matt. 5:45-48)

> [45] *so that you may be sons of your Father who is in heaven; for He causes His sun to rise on the evil and the good, and sends rain on the righteous and the unrighteous.* [46] *For if you love those who love you, what reward do you have? Do not even the tax collectors do the same?* [47] *If you greet only your brothers, what more are you doing than others? Do not even the Gentiles do the same?* [48] *Therefore you are to be perfect, as your heavenly Father is perfect."*

The reason or motivation for praying for our enemies is stated and explained in verses 45-48. The motivation is stated both positively ("so that you may be sons of your Father") and negatively (i.e., so that you will not be like sinners).

---

[5] Ivan H. French, *The Principles and Practice of Prayer* (Largo, FL: The Great Commission Prayer League, 1983), 41.

First, the Lord said we should pray for our persecutors and enemies in order to "be the sons of your Father who is in heaven." This does not mean we actually *become* God's sons by praying for others. Note, He said, *"your* Father." God is already our Father; we do not *become* a son of one who is already our Father! Here "son" is a characterizing term. "Sons of Thunder" was applied to James and John (Mark 3:17) because of their fiery disposition, and the sons of Eli are literally called "sons of Belial," or "sons of worthlessness" (1 Sam. 2:12 KJV; see marginal note in NASB), because they were worthless men. So to be a "son of your Father" is to be characterized by the attitudes of our heavenly Father. Godlike attitudes and actions, in turn, demonstrate that we are truly sons, or children, of God.

By praying for enemies we exhibit the attitude of God, who provides sun and rain for the righteous and unrighteous alike. Such blessings we call common grace, but they are evidence of God's indiscriminate love. It is interesting that Jesus did not say simply "the sun rises" and "the rain falls." Rather, He said God "causes *His* sun to rise" and *He* "sends rain." This looks beyond the action itself to the one who brings it about and the reason He does so: namely, His love.

Verse 46 subtly shifts to a second motivation for praying for our enemies. To love and pray for them is to be like God and not like sinners. Jesus said there is no reward in loving only those who love us. Even tax collectors (and Matthew himself was one!), considered the worst of the worst, did this. Certainly we should love those who love us, but there is nothing special or praiseworthy in this. This is natural and easy, and even the worst of sinners follow this practice.

If we treat with kindness only our "brothers," we are merely doing what the Gentiles do, Jesus said (v. 47). "Gentiles" here is used as a synonym for "sinners." The Romans and other oppressors in Israel's history were Gentiles. "Publicans, Gentiles, and Jews formed separate groups. So did also the Samaritans. ... Fragmentation all around. Hatred everywhere! And as to love? Well, tax-collectors loved tax-collectors. Gentiles cordially greeted Gentiles."[6]

Jesus said to love and thus pray for our enemies. We are not to emulate our enemies and other sinners by reserving our love and kindness and prayers only for those who treat us well. Jesus said there is no reward for doing what the unrighteous do, but He did not speak of the reward for loving and praying for our enemies. The reward for that, it would seem, is being like our heavenly Father. And being like our God calls for us to be "perfect" as our heavenly Father is "perfect" (v. 48). "Perfect" means "complete," and here probably refers specifically to love that is complete. To have the kind of love God has is to have a "complete" love, one that leaves out no person or group, a love that is concerned for and prays even for our enemies, the haters, the persecutors, the liars, the swindlers, and the gossips.

Conclusion

It is indeed striking that the first thing Jesus taught about prayer is to pray for our enemies. His instruction assumed, of course, that his Jewish listeners already prayed. But they needed to see how different Jesus' perspective on prayer was from that of the scribes and Pharisees—those who were considered, and considered themselves, the epitome of righteousness. He is not concerned just with Himself or those who love Him. He is concerned even for His enemies. In fact, it was "while we were yet sinners," that "Christ died for us" (Rom. 5:8), thus demonstrating His amazing love. We are not often called to die for others, least of all our enemies. But we are all called to love them and therefore pray for them. How thankful we are for people who prayed and continue to pray for us. But who will pray for the ungodly, our persecutors, our enemies, if we do not?

Think of someone who hates you or dislikes you. It may be someone you haven't seen in years and may never see again, or perhaps it is just someone who hates Christians in general. Put that

---

[6] Hendriksen, *Matthew,* 316.

person at the top of your prayer list, and faithfully pray for the person. It will change us as we obey the Lord's command; it will demonstrate that we are God's children; and it may have a profound effect on the person we are praying for as we intercede with God on his or her behalf.

6

The Meaning of Forgiveness[1]

(Luke 7:36-50)

IKE GRAHAM

Maybe you have heard of Larry King or have watched his TV show, *Larry King Live.* He has interviewed many preachers, including Dr. John MacArthur, not to mention the many other personalities of stardom or politics. Larry King's twenty-fifth anniversary of broadcasting was in 2010. That year, CNN celebrated by showing his twenty-five best interviews. At the conclusion of that run, CNN had Donald Trump interview Larry King and called it "Donald Interviews the King." Near the end of that program, Trump asked Larry King whom he would still like to interview and what questions he would ask. King responded that he would like to interview Jesus Christ.[2]

Larry reminds me of Simon the Pharisee in Luke 7:36, who invited Jesus to his home for a meal. Chronologically, this event follows Luke 7:35 and Matthew 11:20-30. The now imprisoned John the Baptizer sent messengers to ask Jesus if He really was the Promised One (Luke 7:18-21). Jesus demonstrated His power and authority before the eyes of these messengers by curing diseases, casting out demons, and giving sight to the blind. Then He told the two messengers to report to John what they had seen and heard (v. 22). Immediately, Jesus defended John and His own ministry before the multitudes (vv. 23-34). He concluded by saying that the fruit of their respective ministries vindicates their respective ministries (v. 35). Then, Jesus pronounced

---

[1] The audio message can be accessed at www.sermonaudio.com/ogbc.

[2] Philip Tyson, "Larry Kings Wants to Interview Jesus Christ," Zimbio.com, June 7, 2010. http:// www. zimbio.com/ Larry+King/ articles/ zAf_z3ieBHk/ Larry+King+ wants+interview+Jesus+Christ

judgment upon Chorazin and Bethsaida (Matt. 11:20-30). He concluded this sure warning of coming judgment with an invitation: "Come to Me, all who are weary and heavy-laden, and I will give you rest."

Was the "sinner" of Luke 7:37 in that crowd listening to Jesus explain why the people of Chorazin and Bethsaida would face a more severe judgment? She had heard of the God of Israel and knew what He required, and yet she continued in her sin. The word "sinner" in verse 37 also could be translated, "immoral woman." So she was a woman of the streets, possibly a prostitute. Through the message of Jesus and the work of the Holy Spirit, she was convicted of her sins and came to repentance. That is the point of this section. She was repentant and demonstrated her love to the Lord Jesus by washing His feet with her tears because her sins had been forgiven. This is an important point. Note the verb in verse 47. It reads, "Her sins, which are many, *have been forgiven.*" It's a perfect passive verb. Her sins had already been forgiven, and as a result, she came to show her deep gratitude and love for the Savior.

Jesus' statements and His parable raise some questions for us though, don't they? Questions like: Does a person love more if his or her sins have been many? Are sins forgiven on the basis of love? Does faith save, or does Jesus save? These are the kinds of questions we bring to the text of Luke 7:36-50, humbly asking the Lord to answer for us. We seek His answers from the Word of God in Luke 7:36-50. In these verses, we find five elements that enable us to define forgiveness and understand its relationship to love.

Forgiveness Begins with Repentance (Luke 7:36-38)

> [36] *Now one of the Pharisees was requesting Him to dine with him, and He entered the Pharisee's house and reclined at the table.* [37] *And there was a woman in the city who was a sinner; and when she learned that He was reclining at the table in the Pharisee's house, she brought an alabaster vial of perfume,* [38] *and standing behind Him at His feet, weeping, she began to wet His feet with her tears, and kept wiping*

*them with the hair of her head, and kissing His feet
and anointing them with the perfume.*

In order to receive forgiveness, a person must repent. There
must be a change of thinking about one's way of life and one's
relationship to God. This change in thinking must result in a change
in lifestyle. Through one's change in thinking, that is, biblical repentance, the Holy Spirit gives new desires for the things of God (Acts
26:20).

Let's face it. We have sinned against God. We have transgressed
His commandments and His will. There is an infinite chasm between
us and God, apart from forgiveness in Jesus Christ. The good news is
that in Jesus Christ God stands ready to grant forgiveness to the one
who repents (cf. 2 Cor. 5:18-21). Without repentance, our eternal
destiny is sealed because we are still under the wrath of God (cf.
John 3:36). This should not be difficult for us to understand. If
someone sins against us, we can forgive that person, but it is one-
sided forgiveness. In other words, unless a person repents and asks
for forgiveness, then the person has not experienced the removal of
the sin that blocks his or her relationship with the other person.

Maybe I can illustrate this. In 1830, a man named George Wilson was arrested for mail theft, the penalty for which, at that time,
was hanging. After a time, President Andrew Jackson gave Wilson a
pardon, but Wilson refused to accept it! The authorities were
puzzled: should Wilson be freed or hanged? They consulted Chief
Justice John Marshall, who handed down this decision: "A pardon is
a slip of paper, the value of which is determined by the acceptance
of the person to be pardoned. If it is refused, it is no pardon.
George Wilson must be hanged."[3]

So it is with God. Pardons are not automatic. Forgiveness is not
automatic. A person must repent and come to God with a humbled
heart and changed mind in order to receive God's forgiveness. Have
you done that? Have you called out to God and asked Him to
forgive your sins in Jesus Christ?

---

[3] Liberty Prison Ministries, "The Man Who Refused the Pardon," 2010. http://
members.core.com/~lpm8998/man_who_refused.htm

The same is true in personal relationships. You may have for-given someone for what the person did, but a full restoration in that relationship has not happened until the other person requests and accepts your forgiveness.

This woman did that. She came to Jesus forgiven of her "many sins," and she demonstrated her repentance and gratitude by wet-ting Jesus' feet with her tears, and wiping and anointing his feet with perfume, as the Lord reclined at the table of the Pharisee.

Forgiveness Is Rejected by Self-Righteousness (Luke 7:39)

39 Now when the Pharisee who had invited Him saw this, he said to himself, "If this man were a prophet He would know who and what sort of person this woman is who is touching Him, that she is a sinner."

The Pharisee was shocked by Jesus' willingness to let a "sinner" touch Him. But his sin of self-righteousness was just as bad as her sin. Hers were sins of *commission*. His were sins of both *omission* and *commission*. His pride was a huge sin (cf. Prov. 6:16-17). First, he thought he was better than she was. "He said to himself, 'If this man [Jesus] were a prophet he would know who and what sort of person this woman is who is touching him!'" In other words, "Yuck! I wouldn't let her touch me!" This is the implication of what he was saying to himself. Second, he thought Jesus wasn't even a prophet. Third, he thought he knew what a prophet should be like. After all, he was a Pharisee, and weren't the Pharisees the people of biblical knowledge?

I am concerned that believers too can hold to this same kind of reasoning. We like to camp on 1 Corinthians 15:33—"Bad company corrupts good morals"—to the exclusion of the fact that Jesus spent time with sinners. If we would spend time with people who need the Lord in order to tell them about Jesus, it would benefit us as well as them. It would help our children see how to interact with the lost and not just avoid them. It would also demonstrate that Christians care about non-Christians.

Do you have relatives who do not know the Lord? Invite them over. Spend some time with them. Show them the love of Christ in action. Tell them how they too can be saved from the wrath to come. Explain to your children what is going on and how they also can be good testimonies to the Lord Jesus and honor Him at such times.

Forgiveness Is Revealed By Illustration (Luke 7:40-46)

> *40 And Jesus answered him, "Simon, I have something to say to you." And he replied, "Say it, Teacher." 41 "A moneylender had two debtors: one owed five hundred denarii, and the other fifty. 42 When they were unable to repay, he graciously forgave them both. So which of them will love him more?" 43 Simon answered and said, "I suppose the one whom he forgave more." And He said to him, "You have judged correctly." 44 Turning toward the woman, He said to Simon, "Do you see this woman? I entered your house; you gave Me no water for My feet, but she has wet My feet with her tears and wiped them with her hair. 45 You gave Me no kiss; but she, since the time I came in, has not ceased to kiss My feet. 46 You did not anoint My head with oil, but she anointed My feet with perfume."*

Jesus used an illustration to reveal two important facts about our sin and how we need to see it.

It Is Not Found in the Amount of Sin (vv. 40-43)

Jesus told of two debtors, one who owed a sizable debt and another who owed a vast sum. The major issue in the story, and for the Pharisee, was not the amount of debt. Both Simon the Pharisee and this woman were debtors. The key phrase is in verse 42: "they were unable to pay." Irrespective of the amount, neither could pay the debt. Emphasis needs to be laid on the phrase, "he graciously forgave them both." Simon gets an A in math. He recognized that five hundred is greater than fifty, but he failed to see that even if he were the "fifty" debtor, he still would be unable to pay and would need God to graciously forgive him.

But, someone may argue, Jesus told Simon, "You have judged correctly," so the issue *is* how much is owed. That is a wrong conclusion, because Jesus asked in verse 42, "Which of them will *love* him more?" Jesus did not ask, "Which of them has been *forgiven* more?" Jesus was emphasizing the fact that the sinful woman loved Him more than Simon did because she was more *aware* of her sin. The amount of debt does not matter if one unable to pay. Simon, do you get it?

It Is Grasped in the Awareness of Sin (vv. 44-46)

The real issue is the awareness of sin. Do we really grasp how great our debt to God is? It is infinite because He is infinite. It is eternal because He is eternal. It is spiritual because God is spirit. The Pharisee wasn't getting it because he was spiritually blind. He needed the illustration to get a little understanding. Yet, he missed the point completely. As a result, Jesus really laid into him, didn't He? He said, "Look, your love is miniscule. You didn't even give to me the proper respect that culture demands (water to wash His feet, a kiss of greeting, and oil to anoint the head). But this woman has lavished her love upon Me because she is aware that her sins, 'which are many, have been forgiven.' That is why she loves Me much."

Love Is the *Result* of Forgiveness (Luke 7:47-48)

> [47] *"For this reason I say to you, her sins, which are many, have been forgiven, for she loved much; but he who is forgiven little, loves little."* [48] *Then He said to her, "Your sins have been forgiven."*

The "for" of verse 47 could be translated "in view of the fact."[4] So the translation could go like this: "She loved much in view of the

---

[3] J. P. Louw and E. A. Nida, *Greek-English Lexicon of the New Testament: Based on Semantic Domains* (New York: United Bible Societies: New York, 1996), 89.33.

fact that her sins, which are many, have been forgiven." It also can be understood in English as, "Her sins, which are many, have been forgiven; as a result, she loved much." Jesus' following phrase, "but he who is forgiven little, loves little," points out that Simon might acknowledge that he needed the sacrifices for his sins, but those sins weren't nearly as bad as this woman's. In other words, Simon may have admitted to a little sin, but he really did not see that he was unable to pay his sin debt.

If you're like me, you may have been thinking as Jesus gave it to Simon in verses 44-46, "Yeah! Give it to him, Jesus! The guy's a jerk. He's a hypocrite, and he doesn't even show hospitality!"

But then this thought crosses my mind: "When you woke up this morning, you gave Me no greeting; you offered no prayer; you gave no attention to My love letter to you (the Bible). You went through the day serving yourself. Who really is your God?"

Then Jesus made this statement in verse 47, which makes me wonder if this is why some children who come to Christ at an early age don't get it. The worst thing they can think of is fighting with their brother or sister. Seriously, sometimes I wonder about this. There are times when I reminisce about what God has done for me, and I usually end up in tears. I feel deeply in my heart my heinous sins against God, and I know—I know—that I have been forgiven much. But I wonder how many Christians don't think they have been forgiven much. Maybe you think, "Of course Jesus died for me." Recently, I asked a young Christian man who came to know the Lord Jesus at four years of age if he had ever thought, "Of course Christ died for me!" He responded, "Yes, that is how I used to think." Is that true of you?

Do we really grasp what sinners we really are? I wonder if Jesus showed up right now, what we would do. Would you give Him a "high five"? Or would you pull out your top five questions you've been waiting to ask Him? In Revelation 1:17, the apostle John "fell at His feet as a dead man." When he saw the Lord, Isaiah said, "Woe is me, for I am ruined!" (Isa. 6:5). His self-worth disintegrated before his eyes. All our good things are like stinking, filthy, putrid rags in God's eyes (Isa. 64:6), and Isaiah knew it. Do you know it?

You might be thinking, "But, Pastor, I was saved when I was four! I used no drugs, and the worst thing I did was yell at my mom!" If that is what you think, then you still don't get it. You were saved at four because God knew what kind of sinner you may have become. Being inoculated to the truth, you may have become an addict. You may have become a prostitute. You may have become an alcoholic. By saving you at four, God saved you from a lifetime or years of soul-chaining sin. You have been saved from much. Do you love much? This is what motivates me to serve Jesus Christ! I know from how much He has saved me. Do you know from how much He has saved you?

This woman had been forgiven. Jesus stated this to Simon (v. 47) and then directly to the woman (vv. 48, 50). But forgiveness was not the result of this woman's love; love was the result of her forgiveness. We aren't forgiven because we love Jesus. We love Jesus because He first loved us and showed us our sin. Do you love Him? How much? Do you love Him as much as He has forgiven you?

Jesus Is the *Reason* for Forgiveness (Luke 7:49-50)

> [49] *Those who were reclining at the table with Him began to say to themselves, "Who is this man who even forgives sins?"* [50] *And He said to the woman, "Your faith has saved you; go in peace."*

Jesus is the reason for our forgiveness. "Who is this man who even forgives sin?" the Pharisee's guests asked. Precisely! Only God can do that. But they were blinded by their self-righteousness. Jesus is God. His miracles were the evidence (cf. John 10:37-38). God died in our place; God forgave our sin; Jesus is God. Our faith is the channel through which we receive God's gracious forgiveness, but faith is not the *agent* of forgiveness; Jesus is. It is His death in our place applied to us by the Holy Spirit when we believe that grants us forgiveness.

Conclusion

Let me close by telling you about a modern "sinful woman." Ruth McBride Jordan was a Polish immigrant, the daughter of an itinerant orthodox Jewish rabbi in Virginia. Her mother was a shy invalid who spoke little English and was often physically abused by her husband. Leaving the itinerant ministry, Tateh, as Ruth called her father, opened a general store in which Ruth was forced to work long hours. He treated her as a contribution to his economic success, and he also abused her sexually. Although she loved her mother deeply, she found little solace in her mother's frail and intimidated spirit.

As a result, Ruth spent most of her adolescent years looking for love outside her family. She fell in love with a neighboring African-American boy who often shopped in the store. For the first time in her life, she felt as though someone cared for her. When she became pregnant, she risked the wrath of the small town in which her dad's store was located. Her mom sent her to New York City to spend some time with her aunt, so the problem could be "dealt with."

Returning home, Ruth found that life would never again be the same. As soon as she finished high school, she ran back to New York. There she met Rocky and once again felt loved. She reveled in the warmth and affection of someone who cared for her—only to discover he was a pimp, wooing her to become part of his harem.

Then, Ruth met Dennis McBride. He was the pastor of a Baptist church in New York City. There was something authentic about his affections. This time she was wonderfully loved and was confident of it. Ruth felt safe and valued as he transferred a sense of dignity and worth to her lost and lonely soul. But the secret to her dramatic recovery from a disastrous history did not come from her husband's love, as wonderful as it was, because he died, leaving her a penniless widow in a Harlem flat, overcrowded with kids—twelve of them.

Her strength and resolve came from the Lord Jesus Christ to whom Dennis had introduced her. Years later, Ruth told her son James the secret—the secret that enabled her to rise like a phoenix out of the ashes of her dad's abuse. "I was afraid of Tateh and had no love for him at all ... It affected me in a lot of ways, what he did to me ... but your father changed my life. He taught me about God, who lifted me up and forgave me and made me new. I was blessed to meet him or I would've been a prostitute or dead. Who knows what would've happened to me? I was reborn in Christ. Had to be, after all I went through."[5]

James wrote a book about his mother entitled, *The Color of Water: A Black Man's Tribute to His White Mother*. He also writes this in his book, "Even as a boy, I knew God was all powerful because of Mommy's utter deference to Him, and also because she would occasionally do something in church that I never saw her do at home or anywhere else. At some point in the service, usually when the congregation was singing one of her favorite songs like 'We've Come This Far by Faith' or 'What a Friend We Have in Jesus' she would bow her head and weep. It was the only time I saw her cry. I asked her one afternoon after church, 'Why do you cry in church?' She said, 'Because God makes me happy ... I'm crying 'cause I'm happy!'"

He goes on to say, "Ma was utterly confused about all but one thing: Jesus ... Jesus gave Mommy hope. Jesus was Mommy's salvation. Jesus pressed her forward. Each and every Sunday, no matter how tired, depressed or broken, she got up early, dressed in her best, and headed for church."

Joseph Stowell asks, "How do the Ruths of this world rise above the debilitating effects of brokenness, abuse, deep emotional burdens, bondage, and temptation, to hold their hands high in victory? ... The answer is clear—and the answer holds our only hope. ... [It] is love for Christ so compelling that it drives and defines

---

[5] For the illustration and the quotes here and in the following paragraphs, I am indebted to Joseph Stowell, *I Would Follow Jesus: Writings from the Heart of Joseph Stowell* (Chicago: Moody, 2005), 53-57. Stowell quotes from James McBride, *The Color of Water: A Black Man's Tribute to His White Mother* (New York: Berkeley Publishing Group/Penguin Group, 1996). I am of the Charles Spurgeon philosophy: "All originality and no plagiarism makes for dull preaching."

all that we do—a love that is defined by the life-changing goodness that only He can bring."[6] When our love for Christ moves beyond mere mental assent to a living reality, it motivates us to deal with life in unique and powerful ways, regardless of our circumstances. Friend, I trust that you, whose sins are many, have found forgiveness in the only source of divine forgiveness, the Lord Jesus Christ. Even now, right where you are, you can call out to Him and ask him to forgive your many sins. Will you?

---

[6] Stowell, *I Would Follow Jesus,* 57.

Jesus Was a Jew

JAMES P. COFFEY

The Samaritan woman who met Jesus at Jacob's well progressed in her knowledge of the Lord Jesus, but she first identified him as a Jew: "The Samaritan woman said to Him, 'How is it that You, being a Jew, ask me for a drink since I am a Samaritan woman?' (For Jews have no dealings with Samaritans.)" (John 4:9).

Visiting a Reform Temple

In Jewish tradition, the Sabbath begins at sundown Friday night. One Sabbath night I was at Temple Beth El, a Reform synagogue, for a special service—a commencement ceremony for the young Jews who were graduating from Beth El's religious school. The rabbi, his wife, and many of the parents and adults of Temple Beth El worked diligently to make their religious school a place of excellence. The school went from kindergarten up to the eleventh grade. The nine students graduating from the eleventh grade would become teachers when the religious school began again the next fall.

The rabbi himself taught the eleventh-grade class. He taught the young people how to remain rabbinic Jews while living in a Gentile and Christian world. Assimilation was the ultimate evil.

Some Background Information

There are about six million Jews in the United States, and there are three main branches of rabbinic Judaism in America: Reform Judaism, Conservative Judaism, and Orthodox Judaism. Some would add a fourth: Reconstructionist Judaism. Ultimately, all four of these movements are based on rabbinic Judaism, which is the Judaism that developed after the New Testament era and the two disastrous wars the Jews fought against the Romans (AD 66–73 and 132–135). The utmost expression of rabbinic Judaism is the Babylonian Talmud, which was completed about AD 600. I have interviewed some Reform Jews who believed the loftiest expression of their Jewish faith was studying the Talmud, and they were spending a great deal of money buying the beautiful Schottenstein edition of the Babylonian Talmud. It is sad they didn't have that kind of zeal for studying the New Testament, but, of course, Jesus and the New Testament are not Jewish according to rabbinic Judaism.

Back to Beth El

The youths at Temple Beth El had learned the rabbi's lessons well. One of the graduates spoke to the assembly. He was handsome, intelligent, and well spoken. He thanked the rabbi for all he had taught him. Particularly, he thanked the rabbi for teaching him how to tactfully handle Christian evangelists. The young man said, "This year in high school I had some Christian classmates who tried to convert me to Christianity. As politely as possible and without arguing, I told them, 'No, thank you; I am a Jew, and I follow a different tradition than you. I follow Jewish tradition. Jesus and the New Testament are Christian tradition.' I didn't argue with my Christian friends. We still remained friends. I just politely declined what they were offering."

The people in the congregation smiled and nodded their heads, but I could have cried. Why? Because for two thousand years, rabbinic tradition has declared that Jesus, the apostles, and the New Testament have no connection to Judaism—and thus should not even be considered by Jews. They have been stamped, "Christian! Do Not Touch!"

Matthew's Genealogy

Perhaps that is one of the reasons the apostle Matthew, who was a Jew, began his Gospel with the very Jewish genealogy of Jesus the Messiah. Jesus was the direct descendant of Abraham, Isaac, Jacob, Judah, Boaz, King David, and Zerubbabel (just to name a few of the more significant ancestors of Jesus). Even though Jesus was God's one and only Son, Joseph was His earthly father in the sense that Joseph was the Virgin Mary's husband and therefore Jesus' adoptive father.

The Trump Card

I have spent many years visiting Reformed temples and Conservative synagogues. As a Christian visitor, I have been treated with respect and courtesy. One of the things I have learned while studying Judaism and Jewish history is that if you have a Jewish mother, you are a Jew. This rule is as solid as Stone Mountain. It is an absolute.

You can be a Democrat or Republican, you can be a communist or a capitalist, you can toy around with Buddhism and transcendental meditation, you can visit an Islamic mosque and pray to Allah (I knew a Reformed rabbi who did this in the name of ecumenical cooperation), you can be a Zionist or an anti-Zionist; but as long as you have a Jewish mother, you are a Jew. Having a Jewish mother is the trump card in the significant game of "Being Jewish."

There is only one exception to this rule. If a Jew by birth chooses to believe that Jesus is "the Christ, the Son of the living God" (Matt. 16:16), then he stops being Jewish. Even having a Jewish mother cannot save him—at least from the viewpoint of rabbinic Judaism.

The Jewish Virgin

Of course, Jesus had a Jewish mother. In fact, he had *the* Jewish mother. The Virgin Mary was a Jew and undoubtedly a descendant of King David because (1) the angel Gabriel told Mary her Son would sit on "the throne of His father David" (Luke 1:32); (2) God "had sworn to [King David] with an oath to seat one of his descendants on his throne" (Acts 2:30); (3) Paul, the great Jewish apostle, wrote that Jesus "was born of a descendant of David according to the flesh" (Rom. 1:3); (4) Paul also wrote that Messiah Jesus came from the "Israelites ... according to the flesh" (Rom. 9:4-5); and (5) many Bible scholars believe the genealogy recorded in Luke's Gospel is Jesus' family history through Mary.

Therefore, by the strictest Talmudic standards, Jesus was a Jew because He had a Jewish mother—a royal Jewish mother.

History of Tears

One of the saddest ironies in history is that even though Jesus was a Jew, His apostles were Jews, and the authors of the New Testament were all Jews (except Luke, who wrote under Paul's apostolic authority), over the centuries the Jewish people have ignored their teachings—particularly the doctrine of justification by faith alone (John 3:16; Rom. 3:21-26).

Of course, there have been exceptions to this general Jewish rejection of Jesus as Messiah. By God's grace many individual Jews have trusted the Lord Jesus as their Savior, including such names as Shalem Asch, Victor and Lydia Buksbazen, Alfred Eldersheim, Arthur Kac, Zvi Kalisher, and Lydia Montefiore. (The idea that these people stopped being Jews once they trusted Jesus is absurd.)

It is also sadly ironic that through the centuries people who have called themselves Christians and identified with the church—whose foundation is the Jewish Messiah, the Jewish apostles, and the Jewish Scriptures—have persecuted the Jewish people. The Christian Byzantine Empire persecuted Jews. One anti-Jewish decree even banned Jews from entering Jerusalem. The Roman Catholic Church persecuted Jews in horrific manners. Catholic crusaders murdered whole communities of Jews. The Christian king and queen of Spain drove Jews from the land, even though Jews had lived there for over a thousand years. Edward I, the Christian king of England, ordered all the Jews out of his kingdom. (In one of history's double ironies, it was evangelical Protestant Oliver Cromwell who allowed the Jews to return to the Commonwealth of England.) Christian rulers in Europe forced Jews to live in overcrowded ghettos. The Russian Orthodox tsars of Russia persecuted the Jews like clockwork, and tsarist Russia produced one of the most anti-Semitic tracts ever written: the infamous *Protocols of the Elders of Zion*.

Germany was supposedly a Christian nation, but they let the Nazi devils pass the anti-Semitic Nuremberg Laws and murdered six million Jews in the name of those laws. Some leaders of America, who claimed to be Christians, closed the door on Jewish immigration just as they were trying to flee the acid rain of Nazi persecution. England, also controlled by Christian politicians, closed the door of Jewish immigration to Palestine just before and during the Holocaust. And during the Holocaust, the Vatican said nothing, even though the pope knew Hitler was killing Jews by the millions.[1]

With the Jews' long history of persecution at the hands of nominal Christians, we can understand why a seventeen-year-old Jewish man would tell his Christian friends he is not interested in Christian tradition.

God's Love for the Jews

The apostle Paul loved the Jewish people, his national people, and declared, "I am telling the truth in Christ, I am not lying, my conscience testifies with me in the Holy Spirit, that I have great sorrow and unceasing grief in my heart. For I could wish that I myself were accursed, *separated* from Christ for the sake of my brethren, my kinsmen according to the flesh, who are Israelites" (Rom. 9:1-4).

And Paul promised us that one day, by God's grace, "all Israel will be saved" (Rom. 11:26). So it is not anti-Semitic to wish that all Jews would believe in Jesus. It is not anti-Semitic to desire that all Jews would be born again. It is not anti-Semitic to hope that all Jews would have eternal life. It is not anti-Semitic to wish that all Jews had the very life of God springing up in them "to eternal life" (John 4:14). No, this is just the opposite of anti-Semitism. Moses himself desired for all Israel to have "His Spirit upon them" (Num. 11:29). And Jesus told Nicodemus, the teacher of Israel, "As Moses lifted up the serpent in the wilderness, even so must the Son of Man be lifted up; so that whoever believes will in Him have eternal life" (John 3:14-15).

---

[1] We should not forget, however, that many others who bore the name Christian, both Catholic and Protestant, risked their lives during the Holocaust to save Jews from the Nazi death camps. The State of Israel has even built a memorial to these "righteous among the nations" who lived up to the love of Jesus. And the most fervent supporters of Israel in the world today are American evangelicals. There are millions of them, and they support Israel prayerfully, politically, and financially.

Final Appeal

But how can Jews be saved unless someone will lovingly, patiently, and tolerantly share with them that the New Testament was written by Jews, Jesus was a Jewish Man, and "this Man is truly the Savior of the world" (John 4:42)?

7

How's Your Heart?

(Matthew 13:4-9, 18-23)

TOM TRIGGS

If you have done any traveling, you know that America's landscape holds a wide variety of soil types. The desert states and coastal areas have a lot of hard rock and clay, which is not much good for crop production. Indiana has brown, rocky soil, good for farming but not the ideal all farmers would like. Some states have marshy areas where weeds and tall grasses grow abundantly, choking out any real production. Then there are states like Wisconsin, Illinois, and other Midwestern states that have rich, black dirt that produces in great abundance and consequently feeds millions of people across the country. All these states have something in common: each one has some type of representative soil that characterizes that state.

The same thing holds true for human beings. Each person has something within that is typical or represents the type of person one is. Some people may have a character of clay. Some may be more like brown, rocky soil, and others like marshy areas. Still others may be like rich, black dirt that grows an abundance of produce. Jesus described mankind in this very way. Some are hard as rocks; others are as productive as black dirt.

In Matthew 13:1-9 and 18-23, our Lord describes for us the four types of soil that represent the hearts of mankind. He begins by describing the heart of clay.

Jesus went out from where He was staying to the seaside, and a large crowd gathered, so large that He had to get into a boat and move out a ways on the Sea of Galilee in order to be seen and heard as He taught (Matt. 13:1-2).

His method of teaching the crowd was through parables, and the first of His parables concerned a sower who went out to sow seed in his fields (v. 3). This parable is presented in verses 4-9. In response to the questions of His own disciples, Jesus explained the meaning of the parable in verses 18-23. To begin with we see that the sower (i.e., Jesus Christ; cf. Matt. 13:37) goes out to sow his seed (the "word of the kingdom," v. 19).

A Heart of Clay (Matt. 13:4, 19)

[4] *"And as he sowed, some seeds fell beside the road, and the birds came and ate them up."*

[19] *"When anyone hears the word of the kingdom and does not understand it, the evil one comes and snatches away what has been sown in his heart. This is the one on whom seed was sown beside the road."*

Jesus said some of the seed the farmer sowed fell "beside the road" (v. 4). This packed ground was the footpath or wayside on which the sower walked between the furrows where the seed was planted. This packed pathway also was used by those who passed through the fields while traveling from town to town.

The hardened soil describes the first type of heart (v. 19). It is a heart that hears the word constantly. There is always someone on the footpath, spreading the word in one way or another, and this person hears it. Yet this person constantly rejects the word. He "does not understand it," or literally, does not put it together in his mind.

This person has a closed minded, an unresponsive, calloused heart. He hears the good news of God's Word proclaimed but does nothing with it. God's message, like the seed, lies on the surface and never penetrates into the person's life. It lies in the path of the world's philosophy. Such a hardened heart has no place in it for the good news of salvation and eternal life because it is like a highway, hard and beaten down by the world and the philosophy it follows.

Because the seed remains on the surface, the birds come and quickly eat it. As Jesus explained later (v. 19), the birds are symbolic of evil and particularly the evil one, Satan. He is able to come and take away the word as soon as it is sown because it has not taken root. In reality, this person (usually unknowingly) has been in Satan's grasp so long he never recognizes what is going on. His heart belongs to Satan, and Satan has free rein there.

Alfred Plummer noted that "the unworthy hearer [all of us] becomes less and less able to receive the truth. ... For 'understanding' in scripture is a matter of the heart rather than of the head and the organ which is never used at last loses its power; the ears that never hear becomes deaf."[1]

This is an apt description of what this heart of clay is like. Those with such a heart have gone so long hearing the Word of God and not responding to it that they have become "dull of hearing" and now *cannot* respond. There are many people like that in our churches today. Millions go to church weekly to fulfill their "obligation" but are never moved by the message God's Word brings to them; and because of their hard hearts, they wind up condemned at life's end because they have not accepted the gospel (cf. John 3:36).

A Heart of Stone (Matt. 13:5-6, 20-21)

> [5] *"Others fell on the rocky places, where they did not have much soil; and immediately they sprang up, because they had no depth of soil. [6] But when the sun had risen, they were scorched; and because they had no root, they withered away."*

> [20] *"The one on whom seed was sown on the rocky places, this is the man who hears the word and immediately receives it with joy; [21] yet he has no firm root in himself, but is only temporary, and when affliction or persecution arises because of the word, immediately he falls away."*

---

[1] Alfred Plummer, *An Exegetical Commentary on the Gospel According to S. Matthew* (New York: Charles Scribner's Sons, 1910), 189.

Jesus pictured other seed as falling on "rocky places" (v. 5). This describes a heart that at first shows some possibilities, for immediately a crop "sprang up." The people portrayed here respond immediately to the good news and receive it "with joy" (v. 20). As soon as they hear that there is something to be gained for themselves (which there is), they are thrilled by the message. They immediately receive the good news. They accept what is said, but there is a problem with these people, because their response is shallow and short-lived. There is no spiritual depth, no depth of earth in which the seed of the Word can take root.

It has been said that the person with a heart of stone is actually worse than the first person because his hardness is hidden beneath the surface of a thin layer of black dirt. Actually they are both the same because their end result is the same. This heart responds eagerly to *any* good news, not just the biblical gospel. But because of its lack of spiritual depth, the heart of stone can't retain anything it hears; therefore, the response is shallow, and the message has no effect on the person's life. If there is *any* faith at all, it is only a shadow of the real thing.

One who has a heart of stone has no staying power. Because he responds based on emotion, his life is a jagged graph of ups and downs.

If you want a good example of this, look at many of our mass evangelism campaigns that go on across the country. I have been involved in several of them. Many are blessed by what goes on at these meetings, but studies have shown that *by no means* do all who go forward in these meetings remain faithful. There is a great message, a great appeal to the heart (often the emotions), and a great personal appeal by the evangelist, and great hymns of the faith are sung; but if all who go forward at these meetings are *truly saved*, why are our churches not full? And why is a lot of the preaching so shallow? There is *no depth* to either. Why? Because the appeal is mostly *emotional*.

Emotions are not bad and should not be hidden for the sake of holding back. But we should not let them carry us away to the point

85

where the Spirit of God cannot bless us and give us spiritual depth through His Word.

What pulls a train? It is pulled by a powerful engine; it is not pulled by a caboose. I remember one day my wife and I were in Warsaw, Indiana, at the local Dairy Queen eating lunch. On the hill in front of us was a set of train tracks that ran directly behind our house. While we were there eating, a train went by. Only this train had the caboose first, followed by one or two cars, and the engine last. My wife looked up as seriously as can be and said, "Look. That caboose is pulling that train!" I had the hardest time trying to convince her that cabooses do not pull trains; it was the engine pushing it that made it move.

The same is true in the life of a believer. It is faith in Christ that moves the train. Emotions simply follow at the end of the line of cars being pulled by faith. Don't depend on your emotions to keep your faith strong; neither they nor it will last.

The heart of stone eventually reveals its priorities. In the heat of affliction, when this person's back is to the wall, he turns and runs. He can't take the heat (v. 6). When the sun begins to shine and it gets to 100 degrees F, he withers like the plant that has no root system, and it becomes clear that he has no spiritual depth.

Neither can he take persecution. When it comes time for this person to stand up for what he has so joyously proclaimed and his life, his family, or his job is on the line, he fails to produce in his life and testimony what he has mouthed all along. He backs off and denies what he once said he believed because he depended on his emotions to guide him instead of the Holy Spirit through faith in Jesus Christ. As a result he is ensnared or trapped by the world.

A Heart Full of Weeds (Matt. 13:7, 22)

> [7] *"Others fell among the thorns, and the thorns came up and choked them out."*

> [22] *"And the one on whom seed was sown among the thorns, this is the man who hears the word, and the*

*worry of the world and the deceitfulness of wealth
choke the word, and it becomes unfruitful."*

Jesus said other seeds from the sower "fell among the thorns." In order for anything to grow consistently, there must be plenty of soil; and the proof there is plenty of soil here is the presence of so many thorns or weeds. The heart portrayed by this soil also hears the gospel and responds to it, as evidenced by the fact that at least some of the seed took root and sprouted into a plant. It therefore represents many Christians today.

While there is an abundance of soil, there is also an abundance of preoccupations. The thorns represent worldly cares, riches, and greed (v. 22). And these things choke out the Word. The person preoccupied with the cares of the world is caught up in the wrong pursuits. His heart starts out right. He has plenty of good intentions and follows them for a while. He goes to church, Sunday school, and Bible study and for a while seriously studies the Bible. But for some reason he gets his eyes off of Jesus, and that is all it takes. He begins to see all that the world around him has to offer, and he becomes like Peter, who, while miraculously enabled to walk on the water to Jesus, started looking at his feet and the waves around him and the wind and consequently began to sink into the sea (Matt. 14:22-33).

A sign posted outside a church said, "If you were put on trial today for being a Christian, would there be enough evidence to convict you?" That is not a bad question to ask ourselves. Just how do I stack up against any evidence that might be presented against me? Do my neighbors who are unsaved know that I am different from them? What about my coworkers or classmates or unsaved relatives? Is my testimony for Christ strong enough to stand the scrutiny of an unbelieving world? The world may not believe, but it knows what we should be doing.

This double-minded heart becomes abundantly "unfruitful" (v. 22). Because of the lack of continual spiritual cultivation, this person stops producing any fruit. Here the meaning is that no fruit is brought to the point of perfection or ripens. The potential was there, but because of the greater desire for what the world has to offer (pleasure, position, power, possessions), what had once been a promising, growing Christian has now become stunted and unproductive for the kingdom of God.

William Hendricksen says, "When this person is poor, he deceives himself into thinking that if he were only rich he would be happy. When he becomes rich he deludes himself into imagining that if he were only still richer he would be satisfied, as if material riches could guarantee contentment."[2]

This person needs to ask the Lord to help him get away from this fleeting, dreamy delusion so he can once again become productive for the sake of Christ's kingdom, and God can be glorified in him, which is our ultimate purpose.

A Heart of Black Dirt (Matt. 13:8, 23)

> [8] *"And others fell on the good soil and yielded a crop, some a hundredfold, some sixty, and some thirty."*

> [23] *"And the one on whom seed was sown on the good soil, this is the man who hears the word and understands it; who indeed bears fruit and brings forth, some a hundredfold, some sixty, and some thirty."*

Finally, in Jesus' parable, He said that some seed fell on "good soil" (v. 8). This person is the exact opposite of the previous three persons.

First, this one accepts the gospel. He is not like the one with a heart of clay, who rejects it without exception. He wants to hear.

Second, he understands the gospel. Because his heart is properly cultivated and cared for, he puts it together in his own mind and is not closed-minded; he puts it to work in his life. Third, he asserts the gospel. He not only learns it and starts to become fruitful, but he continues on, witnessing and testifying to the love and power and forgiveness of sin in the person of Jesus Christ because of His death on the cross and resurrection from the grave. As a result, he "bears fruit" (v. 23).

---

[2] William Hendriksen, *The Gospel of Matthew*, New Testament Commentary (Grand Rapids: Baker, 1973), 561.

People with receptive hearts produce fruit and in various amounts. Whether this fruit is viewed as the character traits produced by the Holy Spirit (Gal. 5:22-23) or souls won for Christ, some will produce thirtyfold, some will produce sixtyfold, and others will produce an ever greater abundance of one hundredfold. But all are able to produce. Some have greater abilities than others, but all use their abilities to the utmost.

Conclusion

"Just one letter of the alphabet makes all the difference between us now," said a recently converted girl to an unsaved friend who could not understand the great change that had taken place in her. "You love the world," she said, "and I love the Word."

Which do you love today? Have you rejected God's Word like the heart of clay, an act that, left unchanged, will assure eternal punishment? Are you like the heart of brown dirt, joyful on the surface but hard as rock underneath, rejecting Christ just like the heart of clay and looking for the same end?

Maybe you once committed your life to Christ but have gotten so far off the original track that you have lost your testimony and, like the Ephesian church in Revelation 2, lost your first love: Christ.

What this parable tells us is that without Jesus Christ as your personal Savior, you are bound for hell and eternal punishment.

It also has something to say to Christians. If you are a Christian, you either live in and/or work in a mission field. That field has many different types of hearts/soil in it. As a *minister of the gospel,* you are to sow the seed of the gospel in every area of your life. Some will not accept or receive it at all. Some will act interested at first and then back out. Others will take it and start to grow but then fade away because they let other interests take over their lives, but there will always be some who will accept the gospel, have a great hunger for it, and want you to help them grow all they can; and they, in turn, will tell others and bring them into the kingdom.

Whom can you affect with the sowing of the seed this week? Whom can you talk to who someday may stand beside you in heaven and tell the Lord, "I am here because Valerie, or Roger, or

Sharon, or Dixie, or Alice, or Gerald, or Chuck, or Jan, or Linda, or Kyle, or Erin, or Katie shared the good news of Jesus Christ with me. I got saved because that person courageously spoke the gospel to me"? Sow the seed of the Word this week, and help bring someone into the kingdom.

8

Christis Will Build His Church[1]

(Matthew 16:18)

RICHARD L. MAYHUE

Sir Christopher Wren, the great architect of St. Paul's Cathedral in London, reportedly arrived at the construction site one day and inquired of three different workmen, "What are you doing?" The first replied, "I'm earning a meager living to support my family." The second said he was merely constructing another building. The third had a grander view. He answered, "I'm part of a magnificent project to build the world's most beautiful cathedral to the glory of God." Unless we have the third worker's perspective, sooner or later we will lose our zeal for Christ's first love—the church. By neglect, the church will then fall into disrepair.

Even worse, another contemporary pitfall looms larger; it is possible to have a zeal for the church that is tragically misguided by the ways of the world rather than directed by Scripture. This danger finds modernity more appealing than God's Word when seeking solutions for contemporary problems that face the church. The church that is built this way will be condemned by Christ, not commended.

Unfortunately, when it comes to the twenty-first-century evangelical church as a whole, techniques have replaced truth, style has supplanted substance, convenience outdistances consecration, and modern church growth principles receive more attention than biblical church growth truth. Scripturally speaking, this is not Christ's intended state of affairs for his lovely bride—the church.

---

[1] This chapter is adapted from the introduction of Richard L. Mayhue, *What Would Jesus Say about Your Church?* (Fearn, Tain, Ross-shire, Scotland: Christian Focus, 2001) and used by permission.

This man-centered approach to the church spells out a gloomy future for what ought to be as bright as Christ's glory.

But what can be done to remedy this sad state of affairs? I join Isaiah in shouting, "To the law and to the testimony!" (Isa. 8:20). Evangelicals desperately need to repent of their worldly approach to the church and return to the Scriptures. The church requires a fresh glimpse of her majestic Lord—Jesus Christ; and she needs to become reacquainted with His revealed plan and purpose for the church as outlined in the Bible. She needs to be reminded that Christ will build His church His way.

Can you imagine Christ writing a letter directly to your church as He did to the seven churches of Asia (Rev. 2–3)? What would Christ say about contemporary churches in light of what we know He wrote about first-century churches? This message is designed to help you know Christ's mind concerning the church in general and your church in particular.

Christ's thinking about the church has not changed from what was originally written in Scripture. Therefore, if the church is to regain her former glory, it must be through radical transformation by taking the church back to the basics as outlined in Scripture. Then we all must roll up our sleeves and engage in the hard work of restoring the church to her original beauty according to the biblical blueprint.

Today's Dilemma

Crossroads. Transition. Crisis. Uncertainty. Restlessness. These unsettling words express the perception of many evangelicals regarding the immediate status of the church. Few would disagree that a call for redirection has come to the drifting evangelical church in the twenty-first century. However, there is no current consensus on which route the church should take to get back on track.

In order to appreciate the confusion, consider John Seel's survey of twenty-five prominent evangelical leaders.[2] The leaders ex-

---

[2] John Seel, *The Evangelical Forfeit* (Grand Rapids: Baker, 1993), 48-65.

pressed their views on the general state of evangelicalism at the end of the twentieth century. Eight dominant themes emerged from their less-than-optimistic responses.

1. Uncertain identity—A widespread confusion over what defines an evangelical
2. Institutional disenchantment—A perceived ineffectiveness and irrelevance
3. Lack of leadership—A lament over the paucity of spiritual leadership in the church.
4. Pessimistic about the future—A belief that evangelicalism's future hangs in the balance.
5. Growth up, impact down—A confusing paradox without immediate, clear explanations
6. Cultural isolation—A complete arrival of the post-Christian era
7. Pragmatic response to problems—A drift toward unbiblical approaches to ministry
8. Shift from truth-orientation ministry to market-response driven ministry—A redirection away from the eternal toward the temporal in order to be viewed as relevant

For certain, the decisions made in this decade will reshape the evangelical church for much of the century to come. Thus, the future direction of the contemporary church is a preeminent concern. Unquestionably, the twenty-first century faces a defining moment. The real contrast in competing ministry models should not be the "traditional" versus the "contemporary," as commonly claimed, but rather the scriptural compared to the unscriptural.

"Reengineering the Church" was the theme of a prominent late twentieth-century pastoral leadership conference on how to prepare the church for the next century. As I read the conference brochure, my initial response was, "Why reengineer the church when God designed it perfectly in the beginning?" Shouldn't we inspect the church first and replace only the defective portions? Wouldn't it be best to rebuild the demolished part according to the Builder's original plan? Who can improve on God's engineering?" I concluded the solution is not reengineering but *restoration* to the perfect, original specifications of the divine Designer. The goal of any changes should be a return to the church's biblical roots.

An inspection of the existing church for areas of needed restoration should include such biblically oriented questions as these:

- Have we consulted the *Owner* (1 Cor. 3:9)?
- Do we have the permission of the *Investing Partner* (Acts 20:28)?
- Are we dealing with the *original Builder* (Matt. 16:18)?
- Does the church still rest on the *beginning Foundation* (1 Cor. 3:11; Eph. 2:20)?
- Is the *first Cornerstone* still in place (Eph. 2:20; 1 Pet. 2:4-8)?
- Are we using *approved building materials* (1 Pet. 2:5)?
- Do we employ the right *laborers* (1 Cor. 3:9)?
- Have we utilized the *appropriate supervisors* (Eph. 4:13-16)?
- Are the initial *standards of quality control* still in place (Eph. 4:11-13)?
- Are we continuing to work from the *original blueprint* (2 Tim. 3:16-17)?

Yesterday's Promise

Before wildly plunging ahead to restore the church, we would do well to first look back twenty-one centuries—to the beginning—at the greatest promise ever made on the church's behalf. The Author and Perfecter of our faith (Heb. 12:2), also known as the Shepherd and Guardian of our souls (1 Pet. 2:25), boldly asserted, "I will build My church; and the gates of Hades shall not overpower it" (Matt. 16:18).

We might be persuaded to conclude that a two-thousand-year-old organization, such as the church, would be settled in her identity and purpose by now. However, this is an unwarranted assumption. Unless each succeeding generation returns to Christ's promise in Matthew 16 and to the New Testament building instructions, the church surely will deviate from God's original plan as has been proven conclusively over twenty centuries of church history.

If you seriously reflect on Christ's promise, a number of significant questions should arise.

- To whom do we look when the church is in disrepair—Christ or man?
- Who knows more about the current needs of the church—Christ or man?
- Who can provide better for the church—Christ or man?
- From whom did the original idea of the church come—Christ or man?
- In whom does the church's future hope rest—Christ or man?
- Who built the church up until now—Christ or man?
- Whom do we trust for future directions—Christ or man?
- Who owns and sustains the church—Christ or man?
- For whose glory does the church exist—Christ's or man's?
- Who is the Head of the church—Christ or man?

Because *Christ* is the correct answer to each of these questions, we turn to Matthew 16:18, where Jesus delivers at least seven hallmark principles for building the church. No one should launch out in planning a new church or take on the risk of revitalizing a worn-out church until the defining truths of this Scripture have gripped one's heart and mind.

Tomorrow's Hope (Matt. 16:18)

> [18] *"I also say to you that you are Peter, and upon this rock I will build My church; and the gates of Hades shall not overpower it."*

Hallmark 1

First, Jesus said His church has a *permanent foundation*. Christ passionately pursued the lasting fruit of eternity. In His promise, He explicitly looked to an everlasting legacy. Jesus did not have in mind the temporary, the faddish, or the "here today, gone tomorrow." He pointed to the church as having a "forever" relevance.

"I also say to you that you are Peter, and *upon this rock* I will build My church." The foundation wasn't Peter, because Christ here distinguishes between a moveable rock/detached boulder (the basic meaning of the names Cephas and Peter) and the unshakeable, immovable foundation suitable for the church. The word Christ used for "rock" means bedrock or mass of rocks, like that used by the wise builder (Matt. 7:24-25).

What or who, then, is the rock? The Old Testament pictures God as a rock in whom we find strength and refuge.

> *There is no one holy like the LORD,*
> *Indeed, there is no one besides You,*
> *Nor is there any rock like our God.* (1 Sam. 2:2)

> *The LORD is my rock and my fortress and my deliverer,*
> *My God, my rock, in whom I take refuge.* (Ps. 18:2)

> *For who is God, but the LORD?*
> *And who is a rock, except our God?* (Ps. 18:31)

Paul identifies Christ as the rock in the wilderness (1 Cor. 10:4). And earlier in 1 Corinthians (3:11), the apostle wrote, "For no man can lay a foundation other than the one which is laid, which is Jesus Christ."

Interestingly, just one verse earlier Paul had claimed, "I laid a foundation." How did Paul "lay" Christ as the foundation? Obviously, it had to be in his preaching of Christ (1 Cor. 2:1-2). Now, if Paul's testimony of Christ is the foundation that no one else can lay, then it seems best to understand the "bedrock foundation" of the church as Peter's testimony of Christ, "You are the Christ, the Son of the living God" (Matt. 16:16). Remember, this declaration by Peter prompted Jesus' promise.

Since it is virtually impossible to separate the testimony of Christ from the reality of Christ, we can identify the "rock" as Christ Himself in the fullness of His deity, His role as redeemer, and His headship in the church. Christ alone is the rock of redemption upon which the church is being built (Acts 4:11-12).

Hallmark 2

Second, Christ promised His *personal involvement*. He said, "*I will build My church*." We have not been left to the task alone. Christ is in us (Col. 1:27), with us (Matt. 28:20), and among His church constantly (Rev. 1:12-13, 20).

Paul told the Corinthian church, "We are God's fellow workers" (1 Cor. 3:9). What a privilege it is to be partners with Christ in building His church. How comforting it is to know He built the church before we arrived and He will continue to build it long after we're gone. Christ's participation proves indispensible in raising up His church.

Hallmark 3

"I *will* build My church," Jesus declared. This is no idle dream about what might be. Christ's confident assertion guarantees that the church has a *positive expectation*. In times like these, when the future of the church looks bleak and its condition uncertain, this powerful promise should buoy our spirits. The church will be triumphant because Christ began building the church with the intention of completing her (Eph. 5:26-27).

Hallmark 4

Jesus claimed that His church will have a *powerful advance:* "I will *build* My church." The church experienced an explosive beginning with three thousand members being added on the first day (Acts 2:41). "And the Lord was adding to their number day by day those who were being saved" (Acts 2:47).

What is contained in one mere sentence in Matthew 16 mushrooms into an expansive reality by the time of John's Revelation. Before the New Testament ends, churches existed across the face of the Roman Empire. They included locations like Rome, Corinth, Thessalonica, Philippi, Colossae, Laodicea, Ephesus, Galatia, Derbe, Lystra, Iconium, Antioch, Jerusalem, Crete, Cyprus, Smyrna, Pergamum, Thyatira, Sardis, Philadelphia, Caesarea, Berea, and Joppa. His building efforts continue to this very hour, everywhere in the world, just as He intended (Mark 16:15; Luke 24:47).

Hallmark 5

Christ bought the church with His own blood and therefore possesses the exclusive *paid-in-full ownership* of the church (Acts 20:28). He said, "I will build *My* church." Christ is Lord; we are His servants (2 Cor. 4:5). Paul wrote to believers in Rome, "All the churches of Christ greet you" (Rom. 16:16). Make no mistake about this—we do not (corporately or individually) have any ownership claim to the church. The church belongs uniquely to its Redeemer (1 Cor. 3:23; 6:19-20). Christ is Head of the church (Eph. 1:22; 5:23). The Chief Shepherd owns the flock that He leads (John 10:14-15).

Hallmark 6

"I will build My *church*." For Christ, the church has a *people-centered priority.* The church comprises an assembly of people who have believed in Jesus Christ for eternal life (Acts 4:32). Jesus uses living stones—individual people—to build His church (1 Pet. 2:5). The mandate of evangelization is to take the gospel to all the nations (Luke 24:47). The goal of edification is to present everyone complete in Christ (Col. 1:28).

The Greek word translated "church" *(ekklēsia)* literally means the congregation that has been called out. The New Testament pictures the church as made up of those who have been delivered out of the kingdom of darkness and transferred to the kingdom of Christ (Col. 1:13). The Thessalonians had turned from idols to serve a true and living God (1 Thess. 1:9). The church has been called into fellowship with Jesus Christ (1 Cor. 1:9). Christ has called His re-deemed out of darkness into His marvelous light (1 Pet. 2:9).

Hallmark 7

Jesus has *promised success* to the church. He declared, "I will build My church; and *the gates of Hades shall not overpower it.*"

How is this success to be understood? In the Old Testament "gates of" is used with Sheol (Isa. 38:10) and death (Job 38:17; Pss. 9:13; 107:18), both referring to physical death. Death is really the only enemy that could "potentially" overpower and defeat the church since the church is comprised of people who shall live, even if they die (John 11:25).

The writer of Hebrews encourages us to know that through death Christ has rendered "powerless him who had the power of death, that is the devil" (2:14). Paul wrote this Christian victory song to the Corinthians.

> But when this perishable will have put on the imper-
> ishable, and this mortal will have put on immortality,
> then will come about the saying that is written,
> "Death is swallowed up in victory. O Death, where is
> your victory? O Death, where is your sting?" The sting
> of death is sin, and the power of sin is the law; but
> thanks be to God, who gives us the victory through
> our Lord Jesus Christ. (1 Cor. 15:54-57).

When Christ builds the church these seven features will be identifiable.

1. Christ as the permanent foundation
2. Christ's personal involvement
3. Christ's positive expectation
4. Christ's purpose of powerful advance
5. Christ's paid-in-full ownership
6. Christ's people-centered priority
7. Christ's promise of success

Who could possibly want to build the church any other way?

Christ's Unfinished Work

Theologians often speak of Christ's *finished work* on the cross, referring to the work of redemption. Christ cried out on the cross, "It is finished!" (John 19:30). Truly, Christ's sacrifice need never be offered again (Heb. 7:27; 9:12). Indeed, redemption is the finished work of Christ. However, more is in view for the church than just Christ's death and resurrection. Dr. Luke wrote his gospel concerning "all that Jesus began to do and teach" (Acts 1:1). Just before ascending into heaven, Jesus told His disciples to be witnesses of Him to the remotest part of the earth (Acts 1:8). Reaching the lost with the gospel and then adding to the church daily until Christ returns is the unfinished work of building Christ's church.

By God-breathed, infallible revelation, Christ has communicated to us what He thinks about the church. The Scriptures particularize what He commends and specify what He condemns. No one need ever be in doubt about how to go about the unfinished work of building Christ's church or what the outcome will be.

In the end, our work in building the church on behalf of Christ will be acclaimed as valuable (the allusion to gold, silver, and precious stones) or worthless (the allusion to wood, hay, and straw; 1 Cor. 3:12). The *quality* of each man's work will be tested by Christ in the end (1 Cor. 3:13). Our eternal reward for service done on earth depends on building the church with biblical excellence in order to please Christ.

In the Academy Award-winning film *Chariots of Fire*, Eric Liddell, famed Olympian and missionary to China, conversed with his sister Jenny on a Scottish moor about the timing of his return to missionary work. His response remains etched in my memory. "I believe that God made me for a purpose—for China—but He also made me fast. And when I run, I feel His pleasure."

Nothing will bring Christ greater pleasure than the building of His church. So, aim your life at the bull's-eye of His pleasure, and you will never miss the spiritual target. You'll not be disappointed, and neither will Christ. Your heart will be filled with a great sense of commitment to building Christ's church His way, a commitment wonderfully expressed by these words:

> *I rise up to worship, I stand to acclaim*
> *The King of all ages, Christ Jesus His name.*
> *I ask you, King Jesus, fulfill this desire,*
> *Ignite me and make me, a chariot of fire.*
>
> *Come rule all my life*
> *Lord Jesus Christ, be Master and King.*

Come rule all my life,
Lord Jesus Christ, be my everything.[3]

---

[3] Author unknown.

9

What Jesus Requires of You

(Luke 9:18-26)

IKE GRAHAM

Many years ago—I think it might have been 1978—I was co-pastoring a rural church with another Grace Seminary student. We visited homes in the community, often on Sunday, and shared the gospel with the residents. On one particular Sunday, we came to the home of a young couple. They invited us into their living room, and we shared the gospel with them. I asked them if they would like to believe in Jesus. They said yes, and I led them in prayer.

After praying, I began to explain what God now wanted them to do. I explained how they needed to read their Bible daily in order to grow spiritually. I explained how they needed to be in church with other believers for fellowship, spiritual growth, and service. When I finished, they said, "Well, we're not really interested in those things. We just want to believe in Jesus." They never did come to church. Those two are similar to the people described in John 6. Verse 66 of that chapter reads, "As a result of this many of His disciples withdrew and were not walking with Him anymore." Why? It was because they were fair-weather followers. They wanted to have their stomachs filled, but they refused to commit themselves to Jesus.

People haven't changed. Their attitude is still, "If I can get something without paying for it or making any kind of commitment, fine. Just don't ask me to do anything!" And they have the same attitude toward Jesus: "I don't mind believing in Jesus, but please don't ask me for a commitment!"

This reminds me of the joke about the chicken and the pig. The farmer asked the chicken for a donation for the Resurrection Day sunrise breakfast. She gave him two eggs. When he asked the pig if he would contribute some bacon, the pig said, "For the chicken, it's a donation; but for me, it's total sacrifice!" That is what Jesus requires of us—total sacrifice. We sing about it: "I gave, I gave My life for thee. What hast thou given for Me?" Do we mean it? We should. After all, it is our reasonable service (Rom. 12:1).

Personally, I have a hard time understanding Christians who will make a commitment to the football team or the school choir or the Lion's Club and then make those commitments more important than the Lord and His church. They will make sure they don't miss a practice or a meeting of those organizations, but the very people Jesus died for become a secondary priority. It doesn't compute.

Following Jesus is not simply a matter of putting our name on a roster, paying yearly dues, and showing up at our convenience. It requires much more. What specifically does Jesus require? What does He ask of those who would follow Him? God provides those requirements for us in Luke 9:18-27. There are three.

Jesus Requires Belief (Luke 9:18-22)

> [18] *And it happened that while He was praying alone, the disciples were with Him, and He questioned them, saying, "Who do the people say that I am?"* [19] *They answered and said, "John the Baptist, and others say Elijah; but others, that one of the prophets of old has risen again."* [20] *And He said to them, "But who do you say that I am?" And Peter answered and said, "The Christ of God."* [21] *But He warned them and instructed them not to tell this to anyone,* [22] *saying, "The Son of Man must suffer many things and be rejected by the elders and chief priests and scribes, and be killed and be raised up on the third day."*

In His Identity (vv. 18-20)

If we, like the Twelve, are to follow Jesus with wholehearted commitment, then we must have firmly fixed in our minds who He is. This is why Jesus asked His disciples first what the prevailing ideas of His identity were and then made His question personal: "Who do you say that I am?" If He is simply another self-professed prophet like Mohammed, then He is not unique, and our faith is no different than any other religion. Indeed, even to identify Him with a genuine prophet like Elijah or John the Baptist is to demean Him. Peter understood Jesus was unique, for He was "the Christ [Messiah] of God."

In His Destiny (vv. 21-22)

Jesus' words here assume His approval of Peter's response, something that is explicit in Matthew 16:17. He warned His disciples about openly declaring this truth at that time; then He went on to explain what that truth meant. What really set Jesus apart from all others was the work He would accomplish when He would be rejected, killed, and raised from the dead.

He died for our sins and rose again the third day. Is your heart committed to this central truth? Have you confessed with your mouth that Jesus is Lord? Do you believe in your heart that God has raised Him from the dead? And are you telling others?

Jesus Requires a Bond (Luke 9:23)

> [23] *And He was saying to them all, "If anyone wishes to come after Me, he must deny himself, and take up his cross daily and follow Me."*

Bond is a good word. A bond is something that ties two things together. It could be a rope; it could be money (bail); it could be an agreement. Jesus requires a bond: a commitment to who He is.

A number of years ago, Robert Schuller wrote a book called *Self-Esteem, The New Reformation.*[1] Allow me to quote John MacArthur regarding this book.

> It was an attempt to replace the gospel, the biblical gospel with a new gospel. In that book, *Self-Esteem, The New Reformation,* Robert Schuller writes: "It is

---

[1] Robert Schuller, *Self-Esteem: The New Reformation* (Waco: Word, 1982).

precisely at this point that classical theology has erred in its insistence that theology be 'God-centered' and not 'man-centered'" ([Waco, TX: Word, 1982], 64). ... He writes further, "This master plan of God is designed around the deepest needs of human beings—self-dignity, self-respect, self-worth, self-esteem" (Ibid., 71). For Schuller, the pearl of great price is genuine self-respect and self-esteem.

He further writes, "If we follow God's plan as faithfully as we can, we will feel good about ourselves" (Ibid., 76). That's the gospel of evangelicalism, it's the feel-good gospel. Feel good about yourself. Then he goes on to say: "God needs you and me to help create a society of self-esteeming people" (Ibid., 79). ... So, in this effort at a new reformation, the first thing you have to do is wipe out classic, God-centered, historic theology, then replace it with a man-centered, psychological, self-esteemed theology, thus making everything in the Bible and the gospel work toward making people feel better about themselves to fulfill their dreams and fulfill their visions.[2]

Personally, I don't plan to join. How about you? Is our great need love of self or love of God? Jesus said the first and foremost commandment is to love God. He didn't even mention self. Love of self will characterize the last days (2 Tim. 3:2). This is antithetical to what Jesus said. And what did Jesus say? Let's look.

---

[2] John MacArthur, *Truth Endures: Landmark Sermons from Forty Years of Unleashing God's Truth One Verse at a Time* (Wheaton, IL: Crossway, 2011), 203. This sermon on Luke 9:23 is titled, "The Starting Principle of Discipleship" and was presented on November 2, 2002. It can also be accessed at http://www.gty.org/resources/sermons/42-119/the-starting-principle-of-discipleship

A Commitment to Separate from Self: "deny himself"

Denying self is not the same as self-denial. Self-denial is often touted by Christians today as foregoing certain pastries, pleasures, or possessions. But denial of self means a complete dethronement of my rights and my authority and a surrender of them to the Lord Jesus Christ. This is where true commitment begins. Do I see myself as God sees me?

It was Isaiah who said when he saw God, "Woe is me, for I am ruined!" (Isa. 6:5). The idea was, "I'm literally disintegrating before my very eyes. My whole self-image is disintegrating; it's going to pieces." In the presence of God he saw himself only as a wretched sinner and pronounced damnation on himself because he was a man of "unclean lips." That's what self-denial is. Am I willing to give up my personal desires for material things, other relationships, or the deep physical desires I experience, all for Jesus? This flies in the face of our modern society with its emphasis on self-esteem and self-love.

Listen to Job's words in Job 42:5-6: "I have heard of You by the hearing of the ear; but now my eye sees You; therefore I retract, and I repent in dust and ashes." Consider 2 Timothy 3:1-2: "But realize this, that in the last days difficult times will come. For men will be lovers of self, lovers of money, boastful, arrogant, revilers, disobedient to parents, ungrateful, unholy" (cf. John 8:31).

The essence of denying self is captured in these words of an unknown author.

> When you're not forgiven or neglected or purposely set aside, and you sting and hurt with the insult or oversight, but your heart is happy and you're content to be counted worthy to suffer for Christ, that's dying to self.
>
> When your good is evil spoken of, when your wishes are crossed, your advice is disregarded, your opinions are ridiculed, and you refuse to let anger rise in your heart or even defend yourself, but take it all in patient, loyal silence, that is dying to self.

When you lovingly and patiently bear any disorder, any irregularity, any annoyance, when you can stand face-to-face with foolishness, extravagance, spiritual insensitivity and endure it as Jesus endured it, then that is dying to self.

When you're content with any food, any offering, any clothes, any climate, any society, any solitude, any interruption by the will of God, then that is dying to self.

When you never care to refer to yourself or to record your own good works, or seek commendation, when you can truly love to be unknown, then that is dying to self.

When you see another brother prosper and have his needs met and can honestly rejoice with him in spirit and feel no envy, nor even question God while your own needs are far greater and in desperate circumstances, that is dying to self.

When you can receive correction and reproof from one of less stature than you and can humbly submit inwardly as well as outwardly, finding no rebellion or resentment rising up within your heart, that is dying to self.

How are we doing?

A Commitment to Sacrifice His/Her Life: "take up his cross daily"

Let's start with what bearing your cross daily doesn't mean. It doesn't mean enduring your mother-in-law or your boss or your broken-down car. It means giving up possible high positions or authority, popularity or fame—your own selfish ambitions and desire for "success." It is identification with Jesus to the point where you are willing to die for Him. It is saying NO to self and NO to safety. It is leaving your comfort zone. Are you at that point? Does this characterize your Christian life?

A Commitment to Submit to Jesus: "follow Me"

Will I follow Jesus the way He wants me to, or will I give Him mere lip service and do as I please? Even children can see through the kind of hypocrisy that merely speaks of following Jesus while ignoring His commands. This is the subject Jesus addresses in John 8:31-59.

The message today in the church is, "Are you unfulfilled? Do you feel your dreams are not being realized? Do you feel emptiness in your heart? Come to Jesus, and He'll fill up your heart, and He'll fulfill your dreams." It's all about getting what you want from Jesus. That's not the gospel.

Here is the prayer of one saint who understood what it really means to follow Jesus: "Lord, high and holy, meek and lowly, let me learn by paradox that the way down is the way up, that to be low is to be high, that the broken heart is the healed heart, that the contrite spirit is the rejoicing spirit, that the repenting soul is the victorious soul, that to have nothing is to possess everything, that to bear the cross is to wear the crown, that to give is to receive. Let me find thy light in my darkness, thy joy in my sorrow, thy grace in my sin, thy riches in my poverty, thy glory in my valley, thy life in my death."[3] This is not adding Jesus to your life as an extra insurance policy. No. It is selling out to Him and making obedience to His commands your lifestyle.

> *For the grace of God has appeared, bringing salvation to all men, instructing us to deny ungodliness and worldly desires and to live sensibly, righteously and godly in the present age, looking for the blessed hope and the appearing of the glory of our great God and Savior, Christ Jesus. (Titus 2:11-13)*

---

[3] From Arthur Bennett, ed., *The Valley of Vision* (Edinburgh: Banner of Truth, 1975); quoted by MacArthur, *Truth Endures*, 204.

Jesus Requires a Bottom-Line Choice (Luke 9:24-26)

> [24] *"For whoever wishes to save his life will lose it, but whoever loses his life for My sake, he is the one who will save it.* [25] *For what is a man profited if he gains the whole world, and loses or forfeits himself?* [26] *For whoever is ashamed of Me and My words, the Son of Man will be ashamed of him when He comes in His glory, and the glory of the Father and of the holy angels."*

Will I Choose Self or the Savior? (v. 24)

In May 2013 when I was in India on one those long road trips with Paul, the Conservative Grace Brethren's director of church planting in the states of Tamil Nadu and Odisha, I noticed a sign on the highway that read: Tirunelveli. I asked Paul if this was the place where Amy Carmichael served. He told me it wasn't far from there. Amy Carmichael was a young woman who chose the Savior over self. She chose to lose her life for Christ's sake. She ended up serving the Lord in Tamil Nadu, India, where she rescued many girls from slavery. While she was there, she wrote a number of poems and books. One poem goes like this:

> From prayer that asks that I may be sheltered from winds
> that beat on me,
> From fearing when I should aspire, from faltering when I
> should climb higher;
> From silken self, O Captain free, Thy soldier who would
> follow Thee.
> From subtle love of softening things, from easy choices,
> weakenings;
> Not thus are spirits fortified, not this way went the Crucified;
> From all that dims Thy Calvary, O Lamb of God, deliver me!
> Give me the love that leads the way; the faith that nothing
> can dismay;
> The hope no disappointments tire; the passion that will
> burn like fire.

Let me not sink to be a clod! Make me Thy fuel, Flame
   of God.[4]

Somewhere I read the following anecdote about Harry Ironside
that illustrates this point well. When Harry was a teen, he parti-
cipated in a street meeting. At that meeting he gave his testimony.
Some of his schoolmates had stopped to see what was going on,
and they watched in amazement. On Monday at school, they saw
him and shouted, "Hallelujah, Harry! Praise the Lord!" Harry said,
"Amen." Others said, "Harry, what are you doing? You will lose your
life in this religion!" Harry responded, "That is what I intend to do."
How about you? Will you give up your life for Jesus?

Will I Choose Dollars or the Only Deliverer? (v. 25)

Completely contrary to the bumper sticker that reads, "Whoever dies with the most toys wins" is Psalm 49:17, which reads, "For
when he dies he will carry nothing away; his glory will not descend
after him." The word "glory" also could be translated "wealth." The
saying, "You can't take it with you" is absolutely true. There is no
profit even in gaining the whole world, if one "loses or forfeits
himself."

Will I Choose Shame or to Shine for Jesus? (v. 26)

God is not ashamed of us (Heb. 11:16)! It's amazing but true!
Jesus is not ashamed to call us "brethren" (Heb. 2:11). So when He
speaks here of being ashamed of those who are ashamed of Him,
He cannot be referring to believers. Unbelievers, especially those
who are "Christian" in name only, are those who are ashamed of
Jesus and of whom Jesus will be ashamed at His coming. The
righteous, however, will "shine forth as the sun in the kingdom of
their Father" (Matt. 13:43).

---

[4] Amy Carmichael, "Flame of God," http://www.crossroad.to/Victory/poems/amy
_carmichael/flame.htm

Conclusion

Years ago as a young Christian, I read the book *True Discipleship* by William MacDonald.[5] It had a profound impact on my life. On pages 33-34 of the 1975 edition, was the letter of an American college student who wrote to his fiancé, explaining to her why he was breaking off their engagement. Following is what he wrote.

> We communists have a high casualty rate. We're the ones who get shot and hung and lynched and tarred and feathered and jailed and slandered and ridiculed and fired from our jobs, and in every other way made as uncomfortable as possible ... We communists don't have time or the money for many movies, or concerts, or T-bone steaks, or decent homes and new cars. We've been described as fanatics. We are fanatics. Our lives are dominated by one great overshadowing factor: The struggle for world communism ... There is one thing in which I am in dead earnest and that is the Communist cause. It is my life, my business, my religion, my hobby, my sweetheart, my wife and mistress, my bread and meat. I work at it in the daytime and dream of it at night. Its hold on me grows, not lessens as time goes on. Therefore, I cannot carry on a friendship, a love affair, or even a conversation without relating it to this force which both drives and guides my life. I evaluate people, books, ideas and actions according to how they affect the Communist cause and by their attitude toward it. I've already been in jail because of my ideas, and if necessary, I'm ready to go before a firing squad.

---

[5] William MacDonald, *True Discipleship* (Kansas City, KS: Walterick Publishers, 1975).

Does that describe our commitment to the Lord Jesus Christ? Colossians 3:4 says that Christ is our life. If Jesus is worth believing in at all, then He is worth believing in heroically. Let's take this young man's words and replace *Communism* with *Christ*. Could you say these words?

> We Christians have a high casualty rate. We're the ones who get shot and hung and lynched and tarred and feathered and jailed and slandered and ridiculed and fired from our jobs, and in every other way made as uncomfortable as possible ... We Christians don't have time or the money for many movies, or concerts, or T-bone steaks, or decent homes and new cars. We've been described as fanatics. We are fanatics. Our lives are dominated by one great overshadowing factor: The Lord Jesus Christ. There is one thing in which I am in dead earnest and that is Jesus Christ. He is my life, my business, my religion, my hobby, my sweetheart, my wife, my bread and meat. I work for Him in the daytime and dream of Him at night. His hold on me grows, not lessens as time goes on. Therefore, I cannot carry on a friendship, a love affair, or even a conversation without relating it to Jesus. He both drives and guides my life. I evaluate people, books, ideas and actions according to how they treat Jesus Christ and by their attitude toward Him. I'm ready to go to jail for Him, and if necessary, I'm ready to die for Him.

How about you? Are you willing and ready to die for Jesus?

Proskuneō and the Deity of Christ in Matthew's Gospel

ROBERT B. LANNING

It is widely acknowledged that Matthew wrote his Gospel in part to affirm that Jesus Christ was indeed the King of the Jews.[1] Not surprisingly, Matthew also affirmed the deity of Christ through his use of the Greek word *proskuneō*.

The verb *proskuneō* occurs sixty times in the New Testament. It means *"(fall down and) worship, do obeisance to, prostrate oneself before, do reverence to, welcome respectfully"*[2] and is the most common word in the New Testament for "worship." In Matthew's Gospel it is used ten different times with reference to the worship of Christ. In reply to Satan's request that Christ *worship* him (Matt. 4:9), Christ quoted Deuteronomy 6:13, thus insisting that God alone should be *worshiped (proskuneō)*. Yet this term is repeatedly used for the worship of Jesus.

The account of the wise men's visit to the Christ child includes three verses mentioning the worship of Christ. First, when the wise men arrived in Jerusalem, they informed the inhabitants of the city that they had come to *worship* the One born King of the Jews (Matt. 2:1-2). When Herod met secretly with the magi, he asked them to report to him after they had found the Christ, purportedly so that he could *worship* Him as well (Matt. 2:8). Then, as the wise men entered the house of Joseph and Mary, they fell down and *worshiped* the Christ child (Matt. 2:11) before presenting gifts to Him. This narrative shows Gentiles coming to Jerusalem to *worship* Christ.

---

[1] John F. Walvoord, *Matthew: Thy Kingdom Come* (Chicago: Moody, 1978), 12.

[2] William F. Arndt and F. Wilbur Gingrich, *A Greek-English Lexicon of the New Testament and Other Early Christian Literature* (Chicago: University of Chicago Press, 1957), 723.

Matthew 8:1-4 recounts Jesus' healing of a Jewish leper soon after delivering the Sermon on the Mount. As he came to Jesus, the leper *worshiped* Him (Matt. 8:2 KJV; the NASB renders it "bowed down before Him") and called Him "Lord" (*kurios* in Greek). Here a sick person acknowledged the deity of Christ.

In Matthew 9:18 a Jewish synagogue official in Capernaum named Jairus (Mark 5:22; Luke 8:41), whose only daughter either had just died or was at the point of death (Mark 5:23; Luke 8:41), came to Jesus and bowed down *(proskuneō)* before Him to request that Jesus might lay His hand on her and bring her back to life. Jesus granted him his request (Matt. 9:23-26). Jairus apparently had confidence that Jesus could even raise his daughter from the dead if necessary.

Matthew 14:22-33 relates the well-known account of Jesus' walking on water to meet the disciples during a storm on the Sea of Galilee. When the disciples witnessed Christ saving Peter from drowning as He walked on the water (Matt. 14:31) and the wind miraculously stopping when Jesus and Peter entered the boat, they *worshiped* Christ (v. 33). They recognized, if only for a moment, that only God could do what Jesus had just done.

Matthew 15:21-28 relates the visit of a Gentile woman from the district of Tyre and Sidon who came to Jesus to request that He exorcise an unclean spirit (Mark 7:25) from her daughter. Christ's initial response was silence (Matt. 15:23), and Jesus' disciples requested that He send her away for her boisterous ways. After Jesus pointed out to her that He "was sent only to the lost sheep of the house of Israel," she bowed down *(proskuneō)* to Him and begged for His help (v. 25). Ultimately, her wish was granted (v. 28). This is one more instance of a Gentile acknowledging Christ's deity.

In Matthew 20:20-28, Salome, the wife of Zebedee and mother of James and John, came before Jesus "bowing down" *(proskuneō)* before Him and making a request of Him with regard to the position of her sons in the coming millennial kingdom. Although Christ declared that her request was ignorant and inappropriate because that decision already had been made by the sovereign choice of

God the Father (v. 23), she had rightly recognized the divine authority of Christ over that future kingdom.

In Matthew 28:9, on the same day the Lord Jesus Christ rose from the dead, He met and greeted the women who had seen His tomb was empty (Matt. 28:1-8). They fell down before Him, taking hold of His feet and *worshiping* Him (v. 9). They knew their risen Savior was God and thus worthy of worship.

Later in that same chapter, and at a later date, the eleven disciples met with Jesus on a mountain in Galilee He previously had designated (Matt. 28:16). When they saw Him, although some were still doubtful about His resurrection, the rest *worshiped* Him (v. 17).

Matthew's repeated use of the word *proskuneō* with reference to Christ, from the time of Christ's childhood until the days of His resurrection appearances, is a secondary theme within his Gospel that clearly reveals the deity of Christ.

10

God Will Save Sinners!

(Mark 10:17-22)

RICHARD L. MAYHUE

Perhaps you can remember when you were saved. For me, it was on a Monday night, April 6, 1970, at Scott Memorial Baptist Church in San Diego. 'B' and I struggled in our three-year-old marriage because I loved my career as a naval officer, and she loved our eighteen-month-old daughter.

Fortunately, our Christian neighbors had built a friendship with us to the point that they started inviting us to their local church. Each time we politely refused. Finally, just to appease them, I said yes to a Monday night family seminar. We figured nothing spectacular could happen on a weekday night at a Baptist church.

That evening we heard a simple gospel presentation. I know I had heard the gospel before, but it had never made much sense; plus, in my estimation, I did not live badly enough to be considered a thoroughgoing sinner.

But this night proved different. Everything I heard computed. All the preacher, Kenny Poure, said had the authority of Scripture. My sinfulness became clear in light of God's holiness—I was lost and needed to be rescued. Christ's death on my behalf and God's offer of eternal life were graciously irresistible. By the end of the service, I figured the only logical thing to do was to accept what I so clearly needed and what God had so mercifully provided, and so I did. P.S., so did 'B.'

If you had asked me immediately after the service what had happened, I would have reported that I heard the facts, I considered the alternatives, and I wisely chose eternal life in Christ over eternal damnation in hell. At that time, it seemed as if the whole event revolved around and depended on me.

Over the years, however, Scripture has taught me that God played the major role that night and, at best, I responded in a minor way.

In as clear and basic a way as possible, we want to review the fundamentals of salvation from God's perspective, so that we can understand what happened to us, who did what, and, most important, how salvation has changed us.

The Rich Young Ruler (Mark 10:17-22)

> [17] *As He was setting out on a journey, a man ran up to Him and knelt before Him, and asked Him, "Good Teacher, what shall I do to inherit eternal life?"* [18] *And Jesus said to him, "Why do you call Me good? No one is good except God alone.* [19] *"You know the commandments, 'DO NOT MURDER, DO NOT COMMIT ADULTERY, DO NOT STEAL, DO NOT BEAR FALSE WITNESS, Do not defraud, HONOR YOUR FATHER AND MOTHER.'"* [20] *And he said to Him, "Teacher, I have kept all these things from my youth up."* [21] *Looking at him, Jesus felt a love for him and said to him, "One thing you lack: go and sell all you possess and give to the poor, and you will have treasure in heaven; and come, follow Me."* [22] *But at these words he was saddened, and he went away grieving, for he was one who owned much property.*

Let's first look in on a religiously oriented person who erroneously believed, as I did at one time, that salvation depended primarily on himself rather than on God. We both centered our hopes on human achievement rather than divine accomplishment.

The rich young ruler, highly interested in life beyond death, ran with urgency to publicly inquire of Jesus, "What shall I do to inherit eternal life?" (Mark 10:17). Our Lord's answer has baffled people through the centuries because He did not respond with a simple, "Believe on Me and you will have eternal life." Rather, He exposed the young man's counterfeit interest.

The inquirer betrayed his apparent sincerity by four common mistakes people make in regard to the true nature of salvation. First, he would not acknowledge his own spiritual bankruptcy by admitting that he could do nothing to merit eternal life (Mark 10:17). Only God could accomplish his salvation. Second, he did not acknowledge the Lord Jesus as God. He saw Him only as a good teacher who could explain the way of God (v. 18). Third, he failed to recognize and repent of his own personal sinfulness (vv. 19-20). Rather, he extolled the self-righteous virtues of his life from his youth up. Fourth, he refused to accept the exchanged life of following the will of Christ as Savior and Lord, rather than continuing to pursue his own agenda (vv. 21-22).

Don't be confused here—Jesus did not teach a salvation by works. Rather, just the opposite was true. The rich young ruler tried to gain eternal life through human effort; but the Lord, through a series of questions and commands, pointed him to the real heart of the salvation extended by the mercy and grace of God. Receiving the free gift of eternal life involves at least these four elements.

1. Admitting that only God can save us
2. Acknowledging Jesus Christ as God in human flesh—crucified and resurrected
3. Agreeing to our personal sin, which needs God's forgiveness
4. Accepting God's terms of salvation

Jesus' encounter with this young man stands in contrast to other occasions, where salvation occurred because the above truths were involved. Look at these two prime examples.

> *"But the tax collector, standing some distance away, was even unwilling to lift up his eyes to heaven, but was beating his breast, saying, 'God, be merciful to me, the sinner!' I tell you, this man went to his house justified rather than the other; for everyone who exalts himself will be humbled, but he who humbles himself will be exalted."* (Luke 18:13-14)

And he called for lights and rushed in, and trembling with fear he fell down before Paul and Silas, and after he brought them out, he said, "Sirs, what must I do to be saved?" They said, "Believe in the Lord Jesus, and you will be saved, you and your household."... And he brought them into his house and set food before them, and rejoiced greatly, having believed in God with his whole household. (Acts 16:29-31, 34)

The life of Paul unmistakably illustrates this point. Paul and the rich young ruler both thought identically about salvation in their youth. Before Paul met Christ, he approached salvation from a self-righteous perspective. He thought God owed him eternal life because of whom he had become and what he had done (Phil. 3:4-6).

Later, Paul recognized that he could offer nothing worthy of God and that his best fell enormously short of meriting salvation. At that point, according to Paul's personal testimony in Philippians 3, he counted his religious past to be filthy and as repulsive as excrement. Paul then considered his whole life up to that time as a total spiritual loss in order that he might gain the things of Christ (Phil. 3:7-8).

Until then he had held to a form of godliness but denied its power (2 Tim. 3:5). Now Paul turned his back on self-righteousness through human achievement and by faith embraced Christ's righteousness through God's accomplishment. In so doing, he inherited eternal life (Phil. 3:9-11).

For confirmation of this analysis, reflect back on the historical descriptions of Paul's salvation (Acts 9:3-9; 22:6-11; 26:12-20). In the Acts 9 account, Paul acknowledged Christ's lordship and obeyed His instructions. Acts 22:10 informs us that Paul asked, "What shall I do, Lord?"—similar in words to the rich young ruler's question but quite different in meaning. Paul actually submitted to the will of the One he called Lord. "I did not prove disobedient to the heavenly vision" summarizes Paul's response to God's demands (Acts 26:19).

Paul gave up everything of self and this life in exchange for embracing everything of God and eternal life. Although I could not have explained it at the time, that's exactly what happened to me that April evening on the corner of Oregon and Madison in San Diego. I abandoned self and fully embraced Christ.

Generation

In order to understand why human beings need to be spiritually rescued by God, let's go back to Genesis 1–2. A holy God spoke a holy world and sinless human race into existence. At the conclusion of His six days of creation, "God saw all that He had made, and behold, it was very good. And there was evening and there was morning, the sixth day" (Gen. 1:31).

Into this perfect world He placed a male and female, both created in the image of God (Gen. 1:27). They were not deity, but as God's image bearers they shared some of the divine ability to know and think. Over this perfect world, God gave Adam and Eve dominion, with the freedom to be fruitful, multiply, and fill the earth. They received only one negative command:

> The LORD God commanded the man, saying "From any tree of the garden you may eat freely; but from the tree of the knowledge of good and evil you shall not eat, for in the day that you eat from it, you will surely die." (Gen. 2:16-17)

Imagine a flawless world you could enjoy forever, with only one thing you should not do. That was the world of Adam and Eve. The human race had been "generated" by God's creative energy to enjoy God's blessing forever.

Degeneration

But the story does not end there. Shortly thereafter, Satan deceived Eve (2 Cor. 11:3), and both Eve and Adam violated God's prohibition (Gen. 3:1-6). As God promised, they both died, first spiritually and later physically.

For Adam and Eve, death involved separation. Later on their physical bodies would be separated from their spiritual beings when what we commonly think of as death occurred (Gen. 5:5). But a far more important death took place immediately after they ate—

a spiritual death. At that point, their sin of disobedience separated them from unbroken communion with their holy God. The indications of this are given in Genesis 3:7-13.

1. They were self-conscious (v. 7).
2. They hid from God (v. 8).
3. They were afraid of God (v. 10).
4. Adam blamed Eve for his own actions (v. 12).
5. Eve blamed Satan for her own actions (v. 13).

As a result, God cursed Satan, the woman, and Adam. Then they were evicted from the garden, which housed the tree of eternal life (Gen. 3:14-24).

Let's stop for a moment and put the entire Bible in perspective. Scripture can be outlined around this most important historical occurrence, which resulted in God's curses.

I. Pre-Curse History	Genesis 1–2
II. Curse History	Genesis 3–Revelation 20
III. Post-Curse History	Revelation 21–22

Out of the 1,189 chapters in the Bible, only four speak of a time when the curse of Genesis 3 does not prevail. When the new heaven and the new earth arrive (Rev. 21:1), there will no longer be any curse (Rev. 22:3). The remaining 1,185 chapters contrast man's utter sinfulness and inability to save himself with God's unblemished holiness and His provision in Jesus Christ for human redemption from sin and regeneration to eternal life.

As a result of Adam's sin, the entire human race has been born into sin. Although originally generated in holiness, because of Adam and Eve's fall, the whole human race is now degenerate and eternally separated from God.

> *Behold, I was brought forth in iniquity, and in sin my mother conceived me.* (Ps. 51:5)

> *For all have sinned and fall short of the glory of God.* (Rom. 3:23)

Scripture variously describes this spiritual death as:

1. Darkness of mind that needs to be enlightened by God's truth of redemption (Acts 26:18; Col. 1:13).
2. Depravity of will that needs to be submitted to the orders of God (Rom. 6:11-20).
3. Death of our being that needs spiritual resurrection (Eph. 2:1-7).

The whole human race needs to face the fact that we are born dead to spiritual communion with God. Thus, we have but two alternatives for the future. The first is to be born *again,* this time into the family of God for eternal fellowship.

> *Now there was a man of the Pharisees, named Nicodemus, a ruler of the Jews; this man came to Jesus by night and said to Him, "Rabbi, we know that You have come from God as a teacher; for no one can do these signs that You do unless God is with Him." Jesus answered and said to him, "Truly, truly, I say to you, unless one is born again, he cannot see the kingdom of God." Nicodemus said to Him, "How can a man be born when he is old? He cannot enter a second time into his mother's womb and be born, can he?" Jesus answered, "Truly, truly, I say to you, unless one is born of water and the Spirit, he cannot enter into the kingdom of God. That which is born of the flesh is flesh, and that which is born of the Spirit is spirit. Do not be amazed that I said to you, 'You must be born again.' The wind blows, where it wishes and you hear the sound of it, but do not know where it comes from and where it is going; so is everyone who is born of the Spirit." (John 3:1-8)*

The second alternative is to do nothing and await the second death, which involves eternal separation from God in torment.

> *Then I saw a great white throne and Him who sat upon it, from whose presence earth and heaven fled*

away, and no place was found for them. And I saw the dead, the great and the small, standing before the throne, and books were opened; and another book was opened, which is the book of life; and the dead were judged from the things which were written in the books, according to their deeds. ... This is the second death, the lake of fire. And if anyone's name was not found written in the book of life, he was thrown into the lake of fire. (Rev. 20:11-12, 14-15)

Regeneration

With the seriousness of the second death in mind, we certainly must press on to God's salvation plan for regenerating, or generating a second time, a holy people for eternal fellowship with Him. Degeneration demands regeneration if any human being hopes to enjoy communion with God forever.

The Image of God

God created Adam and Eve in His image (Gen. 1:26-27; 5:1; 1 Cor. 11:7; James 3:9). Sin has marred this glorious image. God in salvation renews and conforms us to the image of His Son (Rom. 8:29), by transforming us into the same image from glory to glory (2 Cor. 3:18).

Salvation not only saves us from eternal separation from God (2 Thess. 1:9-10) but also initiates a renewal back to the original "man in the image of God condition" before the fall of Adam. Just as Christ is the image of the invisible God (Col. 1:15), so we will be changed into the likeness of Christ's perfect humanity (Col. 3:9-11).

God's Initiative

Who is responsible for individual salvation—God or the person? Put another way, did God sovereignly elect us and save us? Or did He act in accord with what He knew we would do? In other words, who makes the first move?

Let me summarize what Scripture teaches about God's role in salvation. I recommend that you look up each passage so you can sense the overwhelming nature of the biblical answer.

God wills	John 1:12-13; Eph. 1:5, 11
God draws	John 6:44
God grants	John 6:65
God calls	1 Peter 2:9; 2 Tim. 1:9
God appoints	Acts 13:48
God predestines	Rom. 8:29; Eph. 1:5, 11
God prepares	Rom. 9:23
God causes	1 Cor. 1:30
God chooses	Eph. 1:4; 2 Thess. 2:13
God purposes	Eph. 1:11
God delivers and transfers	Col. 1:13
God saves	2 Tim. 1:9; Titus 3:5
God makes us alive	Eph. 2:5
God pours out His Spirit	Titus 3:6
God justifies	Rom. 8:30; Titus 3:7

Man's Responsibility

Does this mean God totally overrides the human will to impose His will? The biblical answer is no! There are other passages that teach about man's responsibility for his own sins. Think about these.

> *He who believes in Him is not judged; he who does not believe has been judged already, because he has not believed in the name of the only begotten Son of God.* (John 3:18)

> *It remains for some to enter it, and those who formerly had good news preached to them failed to enter because of disobedience.* (Heb. 4:6)

> *And I saw the dead, the great and the small, standing before the throne, and books were opened; and another book was opened, which is the book of life; and the dead were judged from the things which were written in the books, according to their deeds. And the sea gave up the dead which were in it, and death and Hades gave up the dead which were in them; and they were judged, every one of them according to their deeds.* (Rev. 20:12-13)

People who reject the gospel are held accountable for their sin, rather than being excused because they are the non-elect. While this is humanly impossible to completely reconcile, it nonetheless is what Scripture teaches, and so we must accept it by faith. Jesus was able to hold God's sovereignty and man's responsibility in tension without any mental reservation. Listen to Him preach the gospel.

> *"All things have been handed over to Me by My Father; and no one knows the Son, except the Father; nor does anyone know the Father except the Son, and anyone to whom the Son wills to reveal Him. Come to Me, all who are weary and heavy-laden, and I will give you rest. Take My yoke upon you and learn from Me, for I am gentle and humble in heart; and you will find rest for your souls. For My yoke is easy, and My burden is light."* (Matt. 11:27-30)

Christ's Death

We have redemption through Christ's blood (Eph. 1:7). God made peace through the blood of His cross (Col. 1:20) so that believers might be reconciled to God through Christ. He did not count their trespasses against them but rather against Christ (2 Cor. 5:18-19).

Christ's death was limited in the sense that it does not extend to angels or animals. Nor is it redemptively applied to all humans but only to those who believe in the Lord Jesus Christ according to the glorious gospel.

On the other hand, and in some senses, the atonement of Christ was unlimited in the following ways.

1. It is suitable for the whole human race.
2. It benefits all the elect in salvation.
3. Its message is extended to all in proclamation.
4. It makes common grace available to all people in non-eternal ways.

These brief thoughts suggest that what was pictured as the atonement in the Old Testament paralleled in basic ways Christ's atonement in the New Testament. The yearly atonement in the Old (Leviticus 16) anticipated Christ's once-for-all atonement in the New (Heb. 9:1-28). The atonement also brought common grace to the unsaved in that God's mercy allowed them to live yet another day rather than being immediately judged for their sins.

The Holy Spirit's Renewal

The work of God in salvation vitally involves the Holy Spirit. Most Christians do not know this, or if they do, they haven't fully realized all that this means. Have you ever wondered why we are baptized in the name of the Father and the Son and the Holy Spirit? (Matt. 28:19). It is symbolic identification with each member of the Godhead in relationship to His part in our actual personal salvation. The Spirit of God plays a significant role in salvation.

> *It is the Spirit who gives life; the flesh profits nothing; the words that I have spoken to you are spirit and are life.* (John 6:63)

> *But as at that time he who was born according to the flesh persecuted him who was born according to the Spirit, so it is now also.* (Gal. 4:29)

> *He saved us not on the basis of deeds which we have done in righteousness, but according to His mercy, by the washing of regeneration and renewing by the Holy Spirit, whom He poured out upon us richly through Jesus Christ our Savior, so that being justified*

> *by His grace we would be made heirs according to the hope of eternal life.* (Titus 3:5-7)

The Spirit's work in salvation is sometimes called sanctification, in the sense of the setting apart from sin and to God that takes place at salvation (1 Cor. 6:11; 2 Thess. 2:13; 1 Pet. 1:2). Other terms, including *washing* and *justification,* are used to show the work of God's Spirit in salvation (Rom. 8:6, 9, 23; 1 Cor. 6:11; Gal. 3:2-3, 14; 4:29; 6:8; 1 Thess. 1:5).

You might be asking how someone who is spiritually dead can be made alive, or how someone blind can be made to see, or how someone overcome with evil can be made pure? Jesus illustrated this in the Gospels when He performed miracles of raising the dead (John 11:17-46), giving sight to the blind (John 9:1-41), and freeing people from the evil of demons (Mark 5:1-20). These miracles picture in the physical realm what occurs spiritually in salvation. Salvation begins and ends with God miraculously doing for us what we cannot do for ourselves. It is His work, not ours. It is for His glory and no one else's.

> *For by grace you have been saved through faith; and that not of yourselves, it is the gift of God; not as a result of works, so that no one may boast. For we are His workmanship, created in Christ Jesus for good works, which God prepared beforehand so that we would walk in them.* (Eph. 2:8-10)

God has made us alive; that is, He has raised us out of being dead in sins and trespasses by the regenerating work of the Holy Spirit. As we will see shortly, what God begins with His Spirit in salvation, He continues with His Spirit in the Christian life (Gal. 5:25; Phil. 1:6). These two aspects of the new life—birth and growth—always go together in Scripture.

A New Creation

True salvation is not a decision made today that will bring change only later in eternity. Regardless of how one feels or what one understands at the moment of salvation, it promises to bring with it radical change now: "Therefore if anyone is in Christ, he is a new creature; the old things passed away; behold, new things have come" (2 Cor. 5:17). Whereas I was dead, now I'm alive. Before I was blind, but now I can see. Although I was incurably stricken with sin, God has miraculously cured my transgression problem. Before, I was in darkness, but today I walk in the light. Previously Satan ruled me in his domain; now I am a resident of God's kingdom. Now I am at peace with God, whereas before I was estranged from Him. I am a new creation (Gal. 6:15).

A saved person has laid aside the old self and has put on the new self (Col. 3:9-10). He continues to be exhorted to lay aside the former manner of life, or old self, and put on the new (Eph. 4:24). Because we are "new" in Christ,

- we sing a new song (Pss. 33:3; 96:1; 98:1; 144:9; 149:1; Rev. 5:9),
- we walk in newness of life (Rom. 6:4),
- we serve in newness of spirit (Rom. 7:6), and
- we will receive a new name (Rev. 2:17).

As new creatures in Christ, we are clothed in Christ (Gal. 3:27), and as a result, we are to put on Christlike behavior (Rom. 13:14). This figure of speech involves taking off the filthy rags of our old life and dressing our new life with the garments of a righteous living style.

Conclusion

We close with two great gospel truths. Make sure you have a firm grasp on them.

First, since God initiated and sustains our salvation, true salvation can never be forfeited. We might be short on our personal assurance but never on the God-determined reality of our salvation.

> For I am confident of this very thing, that He who be-
> gan a good work in you will perfect it until the day of
> Christ Jesus. (Phil. 1:6)

"My sheep hear My voice, and I know them, and they follow Me; and I give eternal life to them, and they will never perish; and no one will snatch them out of My hand. My Father, who has given them to Me, is greater than all; and no one is able to snatch them out of the Father's hand." (John 10:27-29)

But in all these things we overwhelmingly conquer through Him who loved us. For I am convinced that neither death, nor life, nor angels, nor principalities, nor things present, nor things to come, nor powers, nor height, nor depth, nor any other created thing, will be able to separate us from the love of God, which is in Christ Jesus our Lord. (Rom. 8:37-39)

Faithful is He who calls you, and He also will bring it to pass. (1 Thess. 5:24)

The second great truth is that since true salvation involves being raised from spiritual death and being made alive in Jesus Christ, then a true believer will show unmistakable signs of spiritual vitality and growth (James 2:14-26).

> *And can it be that I should gain*
> *An interest in the Saviour's blood?*
> *Died He for me, who caused His pain?*
> *For me, who Him to death pursued?*
> *Amazing love! How can it be*
> *That Thou, my God, shouldst die for me?*[1]

---

[1] Charles Wesley, "And Can It Be?" stanza 1.

11

I Am the Resurrection and the Life

(John 11:17-27)

IVAN FRENCH

We are going to look at the great promise of the Lord Jesus that though we may as believers pass through the experience we call death, there is no real ultimate death for the child of God.

It was Andrew Murray, a great preacher from South Africa, who said, "Beware in your praying above everything else of limiting God not only by unbelief but by fancying that you know what he can do. Expect unexpected things above all that we ask or think."[1] I like that: Expect unexpected things above all that we ask or think. Isn't it true of most of us that when we pray, we somehow have it worked out how God is going to, or should, answer that prayer—or even by what means He will answer that prayer?

We have a little illustration of this limitation that we tend to put on God in our passage. Jesus was about a day's journey from Bethany, a little village outside the city of Jerusalem, where Mary, Martha, and Lazarus lived. Lazarus became ill and died that same day. We can pick that up from the time notes in the passage. The messenger Mary and Martha sent was already on his way to where Jesus was in the Jordan area (John 11:3). And when Jesus got the message, He stayed there another two days before He started out for Bethany (vv. 6-7). It took another full day for Him to get there, and by that time Lazarus had been dead for four days (v. 17).

---

[1] Andrew Murray, *The Ministry of Intercession: A Plea for More Prayer* (1898; reprint, Renaissance Classics, 2012), 138.

The disciples weren't a bit excited about going back. They reminded Jesus that the Jews had sought to stone Him in Judea and asked, "Are You going there again?" (v. 8). It was true. Things were dangerous for Jesus around Jerusalem. When He said to these men, "Are there not twelve hours in the day?" (v. 9), He was saying to them, "For one who is walking in the will of God, there is no real danger until his work is done." But when poor old morose Thomas, who had that propensity of looking on the dark side of everything, saw that Jesus was determined to go, he said, "Let us also go, so that we may die with him" (v. 16). He already had his casket picked out, I suppose, and had decided what kind of funeral he was going to have.

My point is this: The apostles' expectations of Jesus were entirely too low. They thought they knew Him well and loved Him, but they had not yet grasped the extent of His power. They didn't understand yet what His purpose was, though He had told them repeatedly that He must go to Jerusalem and there be betrayed by the elders and chief priests and be killed and on the third day rise again (cf. Matt. 16:21; 17:22-23; 20:18-19). But now Jesus tells them, "We are going back to Jerusalem, and on the human level our lives will be in danger. But that's not the whole story."

In the passage before us, we find Jesus and His men arriving in Bethany—a little village just over the brow of the Mount of Olives and about two miles from the city of Jerusalem. There are three movements of thought. We are introduced immediately to the *impossible situation*. Here's a man who has been dead four days. He has been dead so long that by all normal expectations, the process of decay has already set in. And then we have in Martha's greeting to the Lord Jesus what I call a *reproachful salutation,* a greeting that has some mixed elements in it. And then in response to the little dialogue with Martha, there is Jesus' *glorious revelation* of Himself, another one of the great "I am" sayings of the Lord: "I am the resurrection and the life."

The Impossible Situation (John 11:17-19)

> *17 So when Jesus came, He found that he had already been in the tomb four days. 18 Now Bethany was near Jerusalem, about two miles off; 19 and many of the Jews had come to Martha and Mary, to console them concerning their brother.*

Let's look briefly at the impossible situation. Lazarus had been dead for four days. It may be that one of the reasons Jesus allowed this period of time to elapse before He came was a current Jewish belief—actually a superstition—that was quite widespread at that time. It was thought the spirit of a dead person hovered around for about three days after death with the hope that it might enter back into the body. It is not clear how much that entered into His actions, but Jesus was going to make sure, not only in the physical realm but also in the realm of superstition, that Lazarus was dead. There was no more hope that this man could come back to life. No one had ever heard of one dead this long being revived.

The apostles of our Lord knew something about His power to raise from the dead. Some of them had been with Him when He had raised the little daughter of Jairus, but she had been dead only a little while (Luke 8:40-42, 49-56). And some of them were with Him when He touched the body of the widow's son in Nain (Luke 7:11-17). But again, he had been dead only a little while, because it was the custom of that day to bury a person the same day he or she died.

The hopelessness of the situation is emphasized further by the presence of mourners. It is possible these were professional mourners, which were not uncommon in that day, but it seems doubtful. When Jesus arrived there were many people who were still at the home of Mary and Martha, joining them in their grief over the death of their brother. This may suggest they were a family of some influence.

When we look at the physical condition of Lazarus, at the superstition that may have been in view, and at the mourners not shedding one ray of hope on the whole situation, we recognize that Jesus was facing an impossible situation.

He delights in impossible situations, however. Indeed, many of us can recount impossible situations we faced that our Lord handled in some marvelous or unexpected way.

A Reproachful Salutation (John 11:20-24)

> ²⁰ *Martha therefore, when she heard that Jesus was coming, went to meet Him, but Mary stayed at the house.* ²¹ *Martha then said to Jesus, "Lord, if You had been here, my brother would not have died.* ²² *Even now I know that whatever You ask of God, God will give You."* ²³ *Jesus said to her, "Your brother will rise again."* ²⁴ *Martha said to Him, "I know that he will rise again in the resurrection on the last day."*

But now as Jesus and His disciples approached the village, Martha came out. Verse 20 says, "Martha therefore, when she heard that Jesus was coming, went to meet Him, but Mary stayed at the house."

Now this was characteristic of Martha. Back in Luke 10, we read that little paragraph at the end of the chapter describing a time when Jesus went to the home of Mary and Martha. Lazarus was away on business, perhaps, because he is not mentioned in that account. But those verses give us a little glimpse of the differing characteristics and temperaments of the two women. There Martha appears to be one who was always busy and bustling, perhaps something of a fussbudget in that she carried on the affairs of the home, for she scolded Mary because Mary was content to let Martha get dinner while she sat at the feet of Jesus.

And so we see now as Jesus approached the city and word came to the women that Jesus was coming, Martha got up and rushed right out to meet Him. She had some things she wanted to say to Him. Mary stayed right there in the house. It may be that Mary's grief had pressed her into a quiet, meditative mood. But Martha wanted to see Jesus. So she came out to where Jesus was, obviously not very far from the city.

"Martha then said to Jesus, 'Lord, if You had been here, my brother would not have died'" (John 11:21). Well, this is an interesting greeting. It's quite a mixture of faith and a bit of reproach. I see some real faith in this, in that Martha realized that sickness and the presence of Jesus were incompatible. She knew that when Jesus was in the presence of illness, He healed that illness. So she had confidence that if Jesus had only been there when Lazarus was gravely ill, he would not have died at all.

There is a word of reproach here as well, however; that is, she was scolding Jesus just a little. She felt that He should have come earlier. He did get the word that same day perhaps, but He stayed where He was for two whole days before He even set out on the journey back to Bethany. I think Martha forgot something here. She forgot that Jesus could heal from a distance just as well as in the presence of the sick one. We see that a number of times in the Gospels. There was the occasion when a nobleman came to Jesus Himself. He had travelled some twenty-five miles to see Jesus. This man had a son who was desperately ill, and he said, "Sir, come down before my child dies" (John 4:49). Jesus replied, "Go; your son lives" (v. 50). The man believed Jesus and went back home. He may have spent the night somewhere, but when he got back home, he was told that his son had been healed at the exact moment Jesus had spoken.

Indeed, Martha forgot some things. She forgot that the power of the Lord Jesus is not limited to His immediate presence. You and I are mighty glad for that today because He is not physically present with us. Yet His power for our lives is just as real as if He were here.

I see something else that indicates Martha had some genuine faith. She knew Jesus had a unique and special relationship to His Father. We see this in her words: "Even now I know that whatever You ask of God, God will give You" (John 11:22).

How many times had she heard Jesus say, "I came down from my Father; I'm going back to my Father"? She had gotten something of the message of the miracles about which she knew. Her faith was still imperfect, but she knew in a very unique sense Jesus had a relationship to God in heaven that nobody else had. And that gave her confidence that whatever Jesus would ask of the Father He would receive—and that is absolutely true! I wonder if there wasn't a lingering hope in the heart of Martha that Jesus would do something now, even possibly raise her brother from the dead. After all, she knew Jesus had raised the dead before, and the idea of resurrection might well have been in her mind.

Do you have your list of questions to ask these biblical worthies when you get to heaven? Martha, what did you have in mind when you said to the Lord Jesus, "I know that whatever You ask of God, God will give You"? Were you hoping He would do for you what He did for Jairus's daughter and raise your brother from the dead? I don't know for sure, but Martha knew something of Jesus. Imperfect and immature as her faith was, it was nevertheless very real.

But there was also something of despair here. Jesus said to her, "Your brother will rise again" (John 11:23). But Martha's response was, "I know that he will rise again in the resurrection on the last day" (v. 24). Even when Jesus told her He would raise Lazarus, she tended to postpone the possibility of that resurrection until a distant time.

I think there is an important truth for us here. Martha had a pretty accurate theology, but she had an imperfect personal faith. Insofar as her knowledge was complete, she was straight in her doctrine, but she did not yet have that absolute confidence in Jesus Christ that at this moment was her need. Can I throw that out as a word of warning? We can be in a church and community where we receive truth upon truth upon truth. That is good and right and will enable us to recite sound doctrine; yet it is still entirely possible for our personal faith in Jesus Christ to fall far short of what it ought to be. You men who are training for the ministry of the gospel, beware at this point. You can come to the point where you can recite all the tenets of theology clearly and plainly. You can recite all the important dates of history. You can conjugate your nouns and verbs and still be cold as stone in your heart and not have a faith in Jesus Christ that is real and vital and enables you to cope with the matters of the moment and gives you peace and overcoming power in your daily life. And what you have you will impart to others. So be sure the truth you are laying hold of leads you to a relationship with Jesus that is real and vital. Martha had a good grasp of some truth here, but it had not yet led her to a relationship with Jesus that was real and vital.

A Grand Revelation (John 11:25-27)

> [25] *Jesus said to her, "I am the resurrection and the life; he who believes in Me will live even if he dies,* [26] *and everyone who lives and believes in Me will never die. Do you believe this?"* [27] *She said to Him, "Yes, Lord; I have believed that You are the Christ, the Son of God, even He who comes into the world."*

And so our Lord laid hold of Martha where she was, and He now led her to a fuller faith in Himself. Here is the grand revelation He gave: "I am the resurrection and the life; he who believes in Me will live even if he dies" (John 11:25).

Let me pause here to say that so many of the great truths Jesus has given us as recorded in Scripture were given to individuals. "You must be born again" was spoken to Nicodemus. "I am He [the Messiah]" was spoken to the woman at the well. And now to troubled Martha He said, "I am the resurrection and the life, Martha; he who believes in Me will live even if he dies."

Martha's intellectual assent to orthodox doctrine now must progress to a real, vital, unlimited faith in the person of Jesus Christ.

The Affirmation

Let us look at that great affirmation for a moment: "I am the resurrection and the life." Jesus preached Himself. It is one of the characteristics of His ministry. It is one of those things that set Him apart from all the founders of the major religions of the world. Many of them gave tenets of what they believed to be truth, but none dared to stand and say, "All truth resides in me. I am the light. Follow me. I am the bread of life. Feed on me. I am the resurrection and the life. Put your trust in me." But Jesus Christ did. Notice what He said. He told us that He *is* the resurrection. Now at this point He was not saying, "I will perform the resurrection." He had already said that.

In John 5:28-29, Jesus said,

> *Do not marvel at this; for an hour is coming, in which all who are in the tombs will hear His voice, and will come forth; those who did the good deeds to a resurrection of life, those who committed the evil deeds to a resurrection of judgment.*

And in John 6:38-40, 44, He said,

> *For I have come down from heaven, not to do My own will, but the will of Him who sent Me. This is the will of Him who sent Me, that of all that He has given Me I lose nothing, but raise it up on the last day. For this is the will of My Father, that everyone who beholds the Son and believes in Him will have eternal life, and I Myself will raise him up on the last day. ... No one can come to Me unless the Father who sent Me draws him; and I will raise him up on the last day.*

In these passages Jesus was saying, "I will perform the resurrection." He is the one who will call people from the graves.

But in talking to Martha, He went a little deeper. He said something we probably cannot fully grasp. He did not say, "I will perform the resurrection," but "I *am* the resurrection." I think He was saying, "All resurrection is in connection with Me. Apart from Me, there is no resurrection." And this certainly was verified by the word of the apostle Paul in 1 Corinthians 15:20, when he wrote, "But now Christ has been raised from the dead, the first fruits of those who are asleep."

Jesus *is* the resurrection. There is now hope for resurrection in the positive, beneficial sense. Jesus was talking about the resurrection of blessing, the resurrection of life, and He was saying that resurrection is in connection with Him. If we are not connected with

Him, there is no hope of overcoming physical death. He is the resurrection. He is the guarantee that when we lay the bodies of our believing loved ones in the grave, that is not the last word.

Second, Jesus said, "I am the life." Christ *is* the life. He is the ultimate source of life. Beyond Him there isn't anything else. Here again he was not saying, "I will give life." He does that as the Creator, imparting life on every level.

"In Him was life, and the life was the Light of men," John wrote (John 1:4). As Creator Christ imparts all kinds of life on whatever level we are talking about. We see Him in action in Genesis 2:7, where we read, "Then the LORD God formed man of dust from the ground, and breathed into his nostrils the breath of life; and man became a living being." That was Jesus Christ, who is the life, who created physical life on that occasion.

Then we read in John 10:28 the words of the Lord Jesus, "I give eternal life to them, and they will never perish." To those who have physical life and place their trust in the Lord Jesus, He gives them eternal life—that which is vital to that part of man that never perishes. This is not physical life only but goes beyond the physical.

Now, again, Jesus presented Himself not as just the imparter of life but as life itself. Was this what John had in mind when later in his little epistle, he wrote, "And the testimony is this, that God has given us eternal life, and this life is in His Son. He who has the Son has the life; he who does not have the Son of God does not have the life" (1 John 5:11-12)?

Therefore, when we sing our grand old invitation song, "If you are tired of the load of your sin, let Jesus come into your heart," we are being perfectly accurate, because it is as Jesus, as a person, comes into the life, that we receive eternal life. For He is not just the giver of life, though He is all of that; He is life itself. So we pause and ask ourselves the question, Is Jesus Christ in my life today?

The Promise

There is a third thing here. Not only is Jesus the resurrection and not only is He the life, but we also are told that one who believes in Jesus, though he passes through the experience of death, will live again. "He who believes in me ... even if he dies"—a clear reference to physical death—"will live." Here Jesus was answering a question that has plagued the human race from earliest times. No one gave it better expression than the archetype of sufferers, the patriarch Job. When he sat in that pile of ashes, scraping his festering sores with pieces of broken pottery, from his soul was wrung that cry, "If a man dies, will he live again?" (Job 14:14). And if there were nothing else in the Old Testament to make you and me glad we were born on this side of Calvary, it would be that question of Job, because it had no answer in his day. It had no clear answer in all the Old Testament economy. The answer to that piercing question of Job found its perfect expression on this day in this little Bethany cemetery, when Jesus said, "Yes, if a man will believe in me, when he dies, he will live again; he can count on it. The grave is not the final answer." And so on this occasion, Jesus threw a brilliant beam of light on that which for centuries had been hazy and cloudy and uncertain. Jesus said, "If you die, you will live again." And He would give a demonstration of that very truth just moments later when He called Lazarus back from the grave.

This is what will happen to all in a day yet to come. Jesus guaranteed this future, bodily resurrection two months later when He Himself came out of the grave. He had promised His disciples, "Because I live, you shall live also" (John 14:19). And this great truth of the resurrection became the central theme of those early apostles. In the book of the Acts, there are twelve major discourses. At the heart of every one of them without exception is the great truth of resurrection.

This truth was the victory cry of the apostle Paul: "But now Christ has been raised from the dead, the first fruits of those who are asleep" (1 Cor. 15:20). It was the reason for Paul's own fortitude and patience and persistence, for he said, "I do not consider my life of any account as dear to myself" (Acts 20:24). Where do we find an attitude like that today except in the heart of that thoroughly sold-out, dedicated Christian. We don't find it out there in the world. People hang on to life just as long as they possibly can. They will do anything to hang on to five more minutes of this life because they don't know anything about eternal life. But Paul could live with a holy recklessness because he knew the grave was not the end of things. So when he got up, battered and bruised, after he had been stoned, he went right on preaching. When he got out of jail, he just went right on preaching. When his back healed up after some of the beatings he had from the Romans officials, he just went right on preaching. He knew that one day he was not going to be able to go on; he was going to die. He also knew that when he died, he was going to go to heaven and be in the presence of the Lord and that one day there will be a resurrection. And because of that, he could look back on his life and chuckle just a little and dare to say, "I do not consider ... my life as dear to myself."

And this great truth of the resurrection likewise has been the reason for the martyrs' courage. We read a statement of it in Revelation 12:11: "They did not love their life even when faced with death." Why have the Christian martyrs through the ages stood firm even in the face of death? Because they knew they possessed eternal life and there is going to be a resurrection and they will have other bodies to take the place of these bodies that wear out and decay because of disease and age and can be killed by the enemy's sword. This is the reason the Christian today does not need to fear death. I am grateful to the president of the college I attended. I don't remember anything else he said at those Wednesday chapels when he preached. But he used to thunder at us, "Young men, you don't have to live, but you must obey God." You don't have to live, but you must obey God. Why don't you have to live? Because there is a resurrection. And if your life is terminated now, the best is yet to come. You don't have to live, Christian friend, but you must obey God in order to enjoy the fullness of the blessing of God.

Then beyond all this, there is still one more thing. Jesus said there is a life that death cannot touch. He said, "Everyone who lives and believes in Me will never die" (John 11:26). Before the word "die," I would like to insert the word "really," for this is the meaning. One who believes in Christ will never ultimately die. You see, the believer has spiritual life—life that goes on no matter what the condition of the physical body might be. The time comes when the physical body is put in the grave, but the life goes on. The spirit is taken into the presence of Jesus, and that gave Paul such a conflict in his own spirit that he could say, "I'm in a conflict between the two, desiring to depart and to be with Christ, which is far better, but I need to stay here for a while and keep on preaching and look after you folks" (cf. Phil. 1:23-24). That hope was so very, very real to him.

This is the eternal life Jesus was talking about. It is life that is marked with peace, for Jesus said, "Peace I leave with you; My peace I give to you" (John 14:27). It is life that is marked with a very special power, so that the apostle could say, "I can do all things through Him who strengthens me" (Phil. 4:13). Now when Paul said that, he didn't mean he would be able to jump over ten-story buildings or stop speeding locomotives with his bare hands or become a nuclear physicist overnight. He was saying that anything that is in the will of God for me, I can do. This is a life with power. And it's a life marked with real joy. Jesus said to His disciples in John 15:11, "These things I have spoken to you so that My joy may be in you, and *that* your joy may be made full."

And so when those fellows went out and endured their persecutions and finally died, they died joyfully. When Paul and Silas were down in the prison in Philippi (Acts 16), they went right on singing, though their backs were aching and their hands were in manacles and their feet were in stocks. They were giving expression to that joy that was part and parcel of the life they had in Jesus Christ. It is a life with a glorious prospect, an unchanging perspective. As such, the apostle had figured it all out. He wrote, "I consider that the sufferings of this present time are not worthy to be compared with the glory that is to be revealed in us" (Rom. 8:18). So he was content to let the sufferings come, let the hardships come, let the deprivations come, because the best is yet ahead.

The Question and Response

After Jesus had so revealed Himself to Martha in these wonderful truths, He appended a little question. The question He drove home to the heart of Martha is the question He would drive home to our hearts today: "Do you believe this?" Do you *really* believe this? To believe is to possess Jesus Christ, for "as many as received Him, to them He gave the right to become children of God, even to those who believe in His name" (John 1:12). The question comes to us persistently, constantly: Do you really believe this? If we do, then all fear of death will be gone; the bondage of fear will be broken. If we really believe Jesus is the resurrection and the life, we can live with the confidence that comes with the knowledge that when the world has done its worst to us, we will still overcome. That is what Jesus was talking about when He said, "These things I have spoken to you, so that in Me you may have peace. In the world you have tribulation, but take courage; I have overcome the world" (John 16:33). He was speaking anticipatively for the next day the world would do its worst to Him and would put Him to death.

If we really believe Jesus is the resurrection and the life, we can adjust ourselves to whatever burdens and cares and problems are our lot, knowing that one day they will be put away from us and out of our memories because of the glory that shall be ours. We will be able, as Paul instructed, to labor steadfastly, knowing that our labor is not in vain in the Lord (1 Cor. 15:58). How could Paul say this? Throughout that long fifteenth chapter of 1 Corinthians, the apostle had been talking about the resurrection of Christ and the future resurrection of believers, which our Lord's resurrection guarantees. And so he is saying, "Keep right on. Keep pressing on with the work you have to do, knowing that your labor is not in vain." It is not in vain, because there is a resurrection coming, at which time the rewards will be realized.

Martha, bless her heart, felt a little rebuked at this point, and I think it was rather softly that she responded, "Yes, Lord; I have believed that You are the Christ, the Son of God, *even* He who comes into the world" (John 11:27). She might have gone on to confess, "I don't know what all that means. I don't understand all the implications of it, but I believe it with all my heart." It was a noble confession. It was a good confession.

There are some great confessions right here in John's Gospel. John the Baptist said, "Behold, the Lamb of God who takes away the sin of the world!" (1:29). Andrew said, "We have found the Messiah" (1:41). Philip said, "We have found Him of whom Moses in the Law and also the Prophets wrote—Jesus of Nazareth, the son of Joseph" (1:45). Nathaniel said, "Rabbi, You are the Son of God; You are the king of Israel" (1:49). The Samaritans, up there in that pagan land, said, "We believe ... and know that this One is indeed the Savior of the world" (4:42). Peter, who had such a hard time walking because he always had one foot in his mouth, said, "Lord, to whom shall we go? You have the words of eternal life" (6:68). Thomas, overcoming all of his doubts and fears, would say, "My Lord and my God!" (20:28). Now Martha, with all the weakness that you and I have, said, "I have believed that you are the Christ, the Son of God, even He who comes into the world."

If someone should ask you this day—someone out on the street, someone in your neighborhood, someone to whom Jesus Christ is a stranger—"What do you think of this Jesus Christ person, anyway?" what would your confession be? Would you be able to say what expresses the reality of your heart and of your life? "I am the resurrection and the life; he who believes in Me will live even if he dies, and everyone who lives and believes in Me will never die. Do you believe this?"

12

The Universal Enemy

(John 11:1-44)

MICHAEL HONTZ

Humans spend much effort in life trying to postpone death. In fact, the entire medical industry is devoted to fighting and postponing death as long as possible. According to a recent Forbes article, the average family of four spent nearly $21,000 on health-care in 2012.[1] The US government spent an additional $8,600 per person on average on healthcare.[2] That's almost $14,000 per person each year Americans spend primarily trying to postpone death. This doesn't include the time and money invested in things like exercise equipment, healthy foods, anti-aging skin creams, cosmetics, hair dyes, and any number of things we use to postpone or cover up the effects of aging. Yet despite all that money and energy, death is an inevitable reality. One author wrote, "We may postpone it, we may tame its violence, but death is still there waiting for us ... Death spares none."[3]

The ugly and cruel nature of death is most apparent when it strikes in a violent manner, such as in an automobile accident, in war, or in any number of diseases that slowly erode away a person's body and/or mind. First Corinthians 15:26 describes death as our enemy. It has been an enemy ever since the first man and

---

[1] Dan Munro, "The Year in Healthcare Charts," *Forbes,* December 30, 2012. http: //www. forbes.com/ sites/ danmunro/ 2012/12/30/2012 -the-year-in-healthcare-charts/

[2] Wikipedia, "Heath Care in the United States," http://en.wikipedia.org/wiki/ Health_care_in_the_United_States. A copy of the full World Health Statistics 2012 report can be downloaded at http:// www. who.int/ gho/ publications/ world_health_statistics/2012/en/.

[3] Joseph Bayly, *The Last Thing We Talk About* (Elgin, IL: David C. Cook, 1973), 11.

woman disobeyed God in the Garden, incurring death as a curse and the consequence of their sin. Ever since, humans have suffered the daily assault of death pulling us closer and closer to the grave.

The Bible teaches us that God sent his Son into this world to deal with man's great enemy once and for all. A passage that sheds light on this mission is John 11:1-44. It reads,

The Request (John 11:1-3)

> [1] *Now a certain man was sick, Lazarus of Bethany, the village of Mary and her sister Martha. [2] It was the Mary who anointed the Lord with ointment, and wiped His feet with her hair, whose brother Lazarus was sick. [3] So the sisters sent word to Him, saying, "Lord, behold, he whom You love is sick."*

Some have questioned the historicity of this account since only John's Gospel includes it. They speculate an event as significant as Jesus' raising a man from the dead would have been included by the other Gospel writers if it had actually happened. While only John records this particular story, Luke records a separate story about the sisters Mary and Martha, which gives evidence outside of John's Gospel of the historicity of these individuals (Luke 10:38-42). Also, John's comment in verse 2 specifying who this Mary is indicates he believed and expected his audience to view these people and events as real and historical. Additionally, an ossuary was discovered in a tomb near Bethany in 1873 with the inscription of Mary, Martha, and Lazarus.[4] This is a curious combination of names considering the etymology of each is different, one being of Greek, one of Hebrew, and one of Aramaic origin. Ultimately, those who question the historicity of this story do so purely out of speculation, not from any historical or biblical evidence.

---

[4] Andreas J. Kostenberger, *John,* Baker Exegetical Commentary on the New Testament (Grand Rapids: Baker Academic, 2004), 326.

The story begins with Mary and Martha sending word to Jesus that His beloved friend Lazarus was sick. They didn't actually ask Jesus to come, and it's possible they didn't expect him to. It's clear from verse 8 that it was dangerous for Jesus to go to Bethany since the religious leaders were seeking to kill Him. However, the women's responses later make it likely they expected Jesus to come upon hearing of Lazarus's illness. It seems only natural that when someone discovers a close friend is dying, he will make every effort to come quickly, especially if he has the power to heal his friend. Thus, it seems natural to read these verses as a request by Mary and Martha for Jesus to come and heal their brother.

The Response (John 11:4-10)

> ⁴ But when Jesus heard this, He said, "This sickness is not to end in death, but for the glory of God, so that the Son of God may be glorified by it." ⁵ Now Jesus loved Martha and her sister and Lazarus. ⁶ So when He heard that he was sick, He then stayed two days longer in the place where He was. ⁷ Then after this He said to the disciples, "Let us go to Judea again." ⁸ The disciples said to Him, "Rabbi, the Jews were just now seeking to stone You, and are You going there again?" ⁹ Jesus answered, "Are there not twelve hours in the day? If anyone walks in the day, he does not stumble, because he sees the light of this world. ¹⁰ But if anyone walks in the night, he stumbles, because the light is not in him."

Jesus Delayed (vv. 4-6)

Verse 6 says, "So when He heard that he was sick, He then stayed two days longer in the place where He was." As we will see, this detail will prove central to the story. Jesus' delay was not accidental; it was intentional. However, without knowing the end of the story, this makes no sense to us. How else would one interpret this response other than a lack of love or concern, and maybe even an intentional snub? By way of application, how often have we felt these same emotions when God doesn't answer our prayers in a timely manner? To us, it doesn't make sense why He would choose to delay. Thus we question His love and His wisdom in the matter. We struggle to trust Him in times like this. As we'll see, these very questions seem to have loomed in the minds of those mourning Lazarus's death.

Jesus Departed (vv. 7-10)

After Jesus' two-day delay, we read that He then departed. In verse 8, the disciples expressed their apprehension about going because the Jewish leaders were looking to kill Jesus. Jesus responded to their concerns in verse 9 by asking, "Are there not twelve hours in the day? If anyone walks in the day, he does not stumble, because he sees the light of this world." Jesus used fig- urative language here, comparing His own impending death to the night. His point seemed to be that He and His disciples must be busy about the Father's will as long as He was alive (twelve hours of the day). There is no safer place to be than in the center of God's will. Indeed, when walking in God's will, it's impossible for one to stumble. Thus, the reality of Jesus' impending death didn't motivate Him to hide away. Rather, He was compelled to be more urgent in carrying out His Father's will.

The Result (John 11:11-14, 17-22, 28-37)

> *11 This He said, and after that He said to them, "Our friend Lazarus has fallen asleep; but I go, so that I may awaken him out of sleep." 12 The disciples then said to Him, "Lord, if he has fallen asleep, he will recover." 13 Now Jesus had spoken of his death, but they thought that He was speaking of literal sleep. 14 So Jesus then said to them plainly, "Lazarus is dead."*

> *17 So when Jesus came, He found that he had already been in the tomb four days. 18 Now Bethany was near Jerusalem, about two miles off; 19 and many of the*

Jews had come to Martha and Mary, to console them concerning their brother. ²⁰ Martha therefore, when she heard that Jesus was coming, went to meet Him, but Mary stayed at the house. ²¹ Martha then said to Jesus, "Lord, if You had been here, my brother would not have died. ²² Even now I know that whatever You ask of God, God will give You."

²⁸ When she had said this, she went away and called Mary her sister, saying secretly, "The Teacher is here and is calling for you." ²⁹ And when she heard it, she got up quickly and was coming to Him. ³⁰ Now Jesus had not yet come into the village, but was still in the place where Martha met Him. ³¹ Then the Jews who were with her in the house, and consoling her, when they saw that Mary got up quickly and went out, they followed her, supposing that she was going to the tomb to weep there. ³² Therefore, when Mary came where Jesus was, she saw Him, and fell at His feet, saying to Him, "Lord, if You had been here, my brother would not have died." ³³ When Jesus therefore saw her weeping, and the Jews who came with her also weeping, He was deeply moved in spirit and was troubled, ³⁴ and said, "Where have you laid him?" They said to Him, "Lord, come and see." ³⁵ Jesus wept. ³⁶ So the Jews were saying, "See how He loved him!" ³⁷ But some of them said, "Could not this man, who opened the eyes of the blind man, have kept this man also from dying?"

As a result of Jesus' decision, Lazarus died before Jesus' departure. Jesus said in verse 11, "Our friend Lazarus has fallen asleep; but I go, so that I may awaken him out of sleep." Jesus continued to speak metaphorically, saying Lazarus had "fallen asleep" and that He must go "awaken him out of sleep." Jesus' disciples assumed He literally meant Lazarus had fallen asleep, and they questioned Him as to why He would need to awaken him (v.

12). Wouldn't Lazarus simply wake up on his own? Jesus then clarified that He meant Lazarus had died (vv. 13-14).

We get our first clue here that Jesus' earlier delay was not due to carelessness or cluelessness on His part. Rather, it was intentional. Jesus announced He was going with the purpose of raising Lazarus from the dead. Nobody else knew Jesus had this in mind. Thus, we read that they all had the same nagging questions on their minds: "Where was Jesus?" and "Why wasn't He here?"

We see this first with Martha. Verses 20-21 read, "Martha therefore, when she heard that Jesus was coming, went to meet Him, but Mary stayed at the house. Martha then said to Jesus, 'Lord, if You had been here, my brother would not have died.'" It's difficult to know for sure whether her statement was made as an accusation against Jesus for not coming sooner or simply a statement of sorrow that if only He had been able to get there sooner, her brother could have been saved. It seems that at least part of her was upset that Jesus hadn't come sooner than He did.

We read in verses 19-20, "And many of the Jews had come to Martha and Mary, to console them concerning their brother. Martha therefore, when she heard that Jesus was coming, went to meet Him, but Mary stayed at the house." In verses 28-32, we read that Martha came back to get Mary to tell her that Jesus was calling her to come to Him. When the mourners saw Mary leave, they assumed she was going to the tomb to mourn, and so they followed her.

In the New Testament Jewish culture, there were three stages of mourning. (1) During the first seven days after one's death, the family wouldn't leave home except to go to the tomb to mourn. The friends consoled the family at home during this time. (2) The next thirty days the family wouldn't leave town. (3) After that, they returned to normal life.[5] This tradition helps to explain why Mary stayed home initially when Jesus came to town. It also informs us

---

[5] Grant R. Osborne, *The Gospel of John,* Cornerstone Biblical Commentary, vol. 13 (Carol Stream, IL: Tyndale, 2007), 165.

why, when she got up to go to Jesus, the mourners followed her and assumed she was going to the tomb.

When Mary got to Jesus, she, like her sister before her, said, "Lord, if You had been here, my brother would not have died" (v. 32).

This sentiment toward Jesus was not limited to Lazarus's family. Even the crowd was wondering, "Where was Jesus when Lazarus died, and why didn't He do something?" Verse 37 records, "But some of them said, 'Could not this man, who opened the eyes of the blind man, have kept this man also from dying?'" We can hear the frustration in their voices. "Where was Jesus? Didn't He care about Lazarus?"

Death elicits many similar questions from people today, particularly when someone dies an unusually violent or painful death, or when a person dies at a young age. We ask, "Where was God when this happened? If God really cared about our loved one, He would have intervened somehow."

In one of his sermons, Chuck Swindoll recounted the story of the 1956 midair collision of two commercial jets over the Grand Canyon. Several people tragically died in the accident. A young minister living in the area was asked to officiate the memorial service. Seeking to provide the audience with comfort, he assured them that God was present and that He cared about those there that day, as well as those who lost their lives in the accident. One man, overcome with sorrow and anger, called out, "If God really cared, where was He when this happened?" The minister paused and thought about the man's question a moment and then said, "Did everyone hear his question? He asked, 'Where was God when this tragedy happened?' The only answer I have is that God was in the same place He was when sinful men took His Son and crucified him to a cross."[6]

It is important for us to remember that while we often don't understand God's reasons for allowing certain things, He is always

---

[6] An audio version of Swindoll's sermon on John 11 can be found at http://www.insight.org/broadcast/library.html.

good and knows what is best and right. In fact, as we look closely at this passage, we see that just as God has a reason for all He does and allows, so too His perfect Son had a very purposeful reason in His delay and His choice to allow Lazarus to die before He came.

The Reason (John 11:15-16)

> [15] *"And I am glad for your sakes that I was not there, so that you may believe; but let us go to him."* [16] *Therefore Thomas, who is called Didymus, said to his fellow disciples, "Let us also go, so that we may die with Him."*

It Was Based on Love

The first thing we should notice about Jesus' reason is that *it was based on love*. Back in verses 5-6, we read this curious statement: "Now Jesus loved Martha and her sister and Lazarus. So when He heard that he was sick, He then stayed two days longer in the place where He was." Verse 6 begins with the word "so." The purpose of the Greek word used here is to show some type of connection back to the previous statement. It's something like a *thus* or a *therefore*.[7] In other words, *because* Jesus loved Martha and Mary, He chose to stay where He was two days longer.

Jesus' love is seen later in the passage as well. In verse 33, we see that He was deeply moved in His spirit. Commentators note how the word translated "deeply moved" refers to anger and agitation, not sadness. One commentator said, "[This word] always speaks of deep-seated anger and does not connote mere emotional upheaval."[8] This begs the question, "What was He angry about?" He

---

[7] The most common usage of the Greek word *oun* is as an inferential particle, "denoting that what it introduces is the result of or an inference [from] what precedes *so, therefore, consequently, accordingly, then*" (F. Wilbur Gingrich, and Frederick W. Danker, *A Greek-English Lexicon of the New Testament and Other Early Christian Literature,* 2nd edition (Chicago: University of Chicago Press, 1979), 593.

[8] Osborne, *The Gospel of John,* 171.

doesn't seem to be angry at the people. It appears instead that He was angry with death itself and the pain and sorrow this enemy was inflicting on those He loved.

Mark Driscoll shares about his first painful encounter with death. He loved his grandfather dearly and would often spend the night at his house. When it got late, his grandpa would tuck him into bed and say, "Sleep well; I'll see you in the morning." Then he'd smile and wink. This, as Mark came to learn, meant, "Once Grandma falls asleep, I'll come get you, and we'll stay up late and watch wrestling together." One day Mark came home to find his mom crying. She shared that Grandpa had died. Mark never considered that his grandfather would die one day; it just hadn't occurred to him. Mark remembered that at the funeral the pastor spoke about how natural death was, how seasons form cycles, and death is just a natural part of the cycle of life. Mark thought it was the dumbest thing he'd ever heard. "Am I the only one who's angry that Grandpa died? How can this pastor act like this is natural?" he thought. He was angry at the whole situation, and the pastor's words only made him angrier.

I believe Mark was right to be angry, though not at God and maybe not even at the well-intentioned preacher. He was right to be angry with death itself. While death is just as common as life, it is anything but natural. God created us to live forever, with a longing for eternity. Ecclesiastes 3:11 says that God has "set eternity in" man's heart. Death is the unnatural result of sin and the curse; it is man's universal enemy. Jesus identifies with people in the anger they feel over death and what it has done to those they loved. Most of us know verse 35 as the shortest verse in the Bible: "Jesus wept." However, many miss the primary object of His tears. For whom did He cry? Was He weeping out of sorrow that Lazarus, whom He loved, was gone? That seems unlikely in light of the fact that He knew shortly He would raise him to life again. I think it's more likely Jesus wept for Mary and Martha and others who were grieving for their brother and friend. He was identifying with their pain that day. In fact, one of Jesus' reasons for becoming a man was so He could sympathize with the whole gamut of emotions experienced at times like this, when a loved one dies (Heb. 2:14-18; 4:15-16).

It Was to Build their Faith

A second reason for Jesus' delay was His desire to build the faith of Lazarus's sisters and the crowd. When Jesus arrived, Lazarus had been dead for four days. If we allow one day for the messenger to travel to Jesus, two days that He delayed, and another day for Jesus to travel to Bethany, this would account for the four days Lazarus had been dead. It would seem, then, that Lazarus died shortly after the messenger left to go to Jesus.[9] This raises a question: If Lazarus had already died prior to the messenger's arrival and speaking to Jesus, why did Jesus feel the need to delay an additional two days before coming to Bethany? Either way, Lazarus would have been dead when he arrived. A study of the Jewish culture sheds some light on this. The rabbis taught that one's spirit hovered around the grave for three days, hoping to reenter the body. But as decomposition began to take place, the soul would depart.[10] Oral law likewise required that if a body needed to be identified, it had to take place within three days of death. Similarly, later Jewish sources attest the rabbinic belief that death was irrevocable after three days.[11] The fact that Lazarus had been dead for four full days removed any doubt that he was dead and had no chance of being revived, apart from an unprecedented miracle. Jesus' delay thus would serve to build in Jesus' followers their faith in His power over life and death.

If we look closely, we'll find this passage is filled with references to Jesus' intention to see the faith of His followers strengthened. Verse 15 says, "I am glad for your sakes that I was not there, so that you may believe."[12] In verses 25-26, Jesus said to Martha, "I am the

---

[9] Ibid., 167.

[10] Ibid., 169.

[11] Kostenberger, *John,* 333.

[12] In Greek, the verb *believe* shares the same root as the noun *faith.*

resurrection and the life; he who believes in Me will live even if he dies, and everyone who lives and believes in Me will never die. Do you believe this?" In 11:41-42, Jesus prayed, "Father, I thank You that You have heard Me. I knew that You always hear Me; but because of the people standing around I said it, so that they may believe that You sent Me." Three separate times Jesus revealed His goal to elicit faith from Mary, Martha, and finally the crowd as a whole.

It Was to Bring God Glory

There is at least one final purpose for Jesus' delay: to bring God glory. All the way back in verse 4, Jesus mentioned that Lazarus's sickness was not to end in death. Such a statement seems to contradict the reality that Lazarus did, in fact, die. The Greek here literally reads something like this: "This illness is not unto (or for) death." One way to understand this is that the ultimate end or goal of his sickness was not to bring about death but something far grander. This fits the actual events, since in the end Lazarus did not remain dead. Jesus went on to say that the ultimate purpose of the illness was to bring God glory. The sickness was "for the glory of God, so that the Son of God may be glorified by it."

We tend to view events from the perspective of how they affect us, either positively or negatively. A real mark of spiritual maturity is the ability to view events and judge their merit by the criteria of whether or not they bring glory to God. Jesus modeled this attitude. He often demonstrated a desire for His Father to receive glory, for His Father's will to be done, even when His own human interests were neglected. This is seen most clearly in the Garden of Gethsemane, as Jesus looked ahead to the cross and said, "Father, if You are willing, remove this cup from Me; yet not My will, but Yours be done" (Luke 22:42).

How exactly would Jesus and the Father receive glory through this event? I believe the primary answer lies in a fifth and final point.

The Resurrection (John 11:38-44, 25, 23-27)

> [38] *So Jesus, again being deeply moved within, came to the tomb. Now it was a cave, and a stone was lying against it.* [39] *Jesus said, "Remove the stone." Martha, the sister of the deceased, said to Him, "Lord, by this time there will be a stench, for he has been dead four days."* [40] *Jesus said to her, "Did I not say to you that if you believe, you will see the glory of God?"* [41] *So they removed the stone. Then Jesus raised His eyes, and said, "Father, I thank You that You have heard Me.* [42] *I knew that You always hear Me; but because of the people standing around I said it, so that they may believe that You sent Me."* [43] *When He had said these things, He cried out with a loud voice, "Lazarus, come forth."* [44] *The man who had died came forth, bound hand and foot with wrappings, and his face was wrapped around with a cloth. Jesus said to them, "Unbind him, and let him go."*
>
> [25] *Jesus said to her, "I am the resurrection and the life; he who believes in Me will live even if he dies."*
>
> [23] *Jesus said to her, "Your brother will rise again."* [24] *Martha said to Him, "I know that he will rise again in the resurrection on the last day."* [25] *Jesus said to her, "I am the resurrection and the life; he who believes in Me will live even if he dies,* [26] *and every-one who lives and believes in Me will never die. Do you believe this?"* [27] *She said to Him, "Yes, Lord; I have believed that You are the Christ, the Son of God, even He who comes into the world."*

The Resurrection of Lazarus (vv. 38-44)

The first resurrection this passage points to is the resurrection of Lazarus. John 11:38-39 reads, "So Jesus, again being deeply moved within, came to the tomb. Now it was a cave, and a stone was lying against it. Jesus said, 'Remove the stone.' Martha, the sister of the deceased, said to Him, 'Lord, by this time there will be a stench, for he has been dead four days.'"

I recently watched a television show about a couple who had bought a house with the goal of fixing it up and reselling it. However, there was a strong stench in the house from the time they bought it. This made it very uncomfortable for the people who worked on the house. As work progressed and they got closer to the open house, they grew concerned over the fact they hadn't discovered the source of the smell, and it was only getting worse. The day before the open house, while cleaning a ceiling vent in the bathroom, someone discovered a dead bat that had gotten in from outside and died there. They were amazed that such a small animal could cause such a putrid odor. Comparatively, imagine the odor of a grown man's decomposing body.

Verses 43-44 say, "When He had said these things, He cried out with a loud voice, 'Lazarus, come forth.' The man who had died came forth, bound hand and foot with wrappings, and his face was wrapped around with a cloth. Jesus said to them, 'Unbind him, and let him go.'" Jesus' command in verse 43 is literally two words: "Here! Outside!" It's interesting that Jesus' words were the apparent means of giving life to Lazarus. Similarly, it was God's words that spoke human life into existence in the creation account of Genesis 1. Some make a distinction between resuscitation and resurrection. Lazarus did not receive a new body, never to die again, as one would in a resurrection. While this is a legitimate distinction, I believe it is still appropriate to refer to this as a resurrection. In fact, I believe this event was intended to prefigure and point forward to the coming resurrection of Jesus Himself. This brings us to the next point.

The Resurrection of the Lord (v. 25)

There are many verbal correlations between the description of the death and resurrection of Lazarus and that of Jesus later in John's Gospel (See John 20). Both use the term "dead man" (used exclusively by John of Jesus and Lazarus). Both stories refer to the men's burial cloths and to a physical tomb with a stone that is rolled away. The story of Lazarus is the climax of the pre-Passion narrative in John's Gospel. The Gospel centers around seven signs and seven "I Am" statements by Jesus. The raising of Lazarus is the seventh and final sign. This story also contains the fifth "I Am" statement by Jesus, when He says, "I am the resurrection and the life" (John 11:25). As such, both His claim and His miracle point to Jesus as the source of resurrection life for all.

Jesus went on to say, "He who believes in Me will live even if he dies, and everyone who lives and believes in Me will never die" (vv. 25-26). These two statements appear contradictory at first glance. First, Jesus says that even though he dies, yet the one who believes in Him will live. Then He claims that this one will never die. The apparent contradiction is probably intentional to elicit from His hearers meditation on these truths. Taking them together, the sense is that even in death, those who believe in Christ will still live. Their spirit will go on living forever; thus they never truly die.

Easter begs the question from all: "Do you believe in Christ?" It is not simply a question of whether one believes He existed. The people in Jesus' context saw and heard Him; there was no question about whether He existed. The issue of their faith went far deeper. The issue revolved around whether or not they believed He was who He claimed to be—God—and whether He had authority over life and death. This brings us to the final resurrection of the last days.

The Resurrection of the Last Days (vv. 23-27)

In verse 23, Jesus told Martha that Lazarus would rise again. Martha conceded that he would rise again in the last day. Jesus did not correct her. In fact, He went on to explain how the truth of the resurrection on the last day applies to everyone who believes in Him. And while Jesus wasn't speaking in Lazarus's case about this resurrection of the last day when He said Lazarus would rise again, He did elaborate on this truth for the crowd around Him. If they trusted in Jesus, even in death they would live. This was the resurrection for which they all could long.

This theme of the resurrection on the last day is something John's Gospel highlighted from Jesus' teaching ministry. In John 5:25-29, Jesus taught,

> *Truly, truly, I say to you, an hour is coming and now is, when the dead will hear the voice of the Son of God, and those who hear will live. For just as the Father has life in Himself, even so He gave to the Son also to have life in Himself; and He gave Him authority to execute judgment, because He is the Son of Man. Do not marvel at this; for an hour is coming, in which all who are in the tombs will hear His voice, and will come forth; those who did the good deeds to a resurrection of life, those who committed the evil deeds to a resurrection of judgment.*

Likewise, in John 6:40 Jesus says, "For this is the will of My Father, that everyone who beholds the Son and believes in Him will have eternal life, and I Myself will raise him up on the last day."

Conclusion

This story of the raising of Lazarus is for all who have ever faced pain from a loved one's death. Our temptation is to think like Mary, Martha, and the crowd, "If only God cared, if He had intervened, this wouldn't have happened. Certainly my son or daughter or spouse or best friend wouldn't have died if God existed or if He were a good and loving God." The grand truth of this passage is this, and don't miss it: God *has* done something! He did something far greater than keeping your loved one from dying. By sending His Son to die and rise again, He conquered death permanently for all eternity for everyone and anyone who trusts in Him. Physical death is a necessary step in experiencing resurrection life. "He who believes in Me will live even if he dies, and everyone who lives and believes in Me will never die."

The motorcyclist Robert Craig Knievel, widely known as "Evel Knievel," became the most famous daredevil on earth during the 1960s and '70s. Jumping over buses and cars earned him over $30 million. He cheated death time and again. During his second performance, Knievel attempted to jump, spread eagle, over a speeding motorcycle. He jumped late, and the motorcycle hit him in the pelvic area, tossing him fifteen feet into the air. He was hospitalized as a result of his injuries. When he was released, he returned to finish the performance he'd begun a month earlier. Over the course of his career, he suffered forty bone fractures, including a broken back seven times. He was in a coma for weeks following a crash at Caesars Palace in Las Vegas.

Even after his career was over, Knievel continued to cheat death. In February of 1999, he left a hospital after being told he had only a few days to live because he needed a liver transplant. On his way home, he received a call from the hospital. A man who had been in a motorcycle accident could serve as a donor. The transplant was successful, and Knievel once again avoided death.

Nobody can avoid death forever, though. In November of 2007, Robert Knievel breathed his last breath. However, even in death, he was able to cheat death. You see, seven months earlier, Knievel announced to a worldwide audience that he believed in Jesus Christ for the first time. He professed his personal faith in Jesus to over four thousand people gathered inside the Crystal Cathedral for Palm Sunday services. He was baptized before the church and TV cameras.[13]

Evil Knievel's life, like the story of Lazarus, leaves us with an important question to ponder. If you were to die today, would you cheat death? Have you ever trusted in Jesus Christ—His death and resurrection—to bring you forgiveness of sins now and eternal life forever? If not, I invite you to do that today.

---

[13] Craig Brian Larson and Phyllis Ten Elshof, *1001 Illustrations That Connect* (Grand Rapids: Zondervan, 2008), 417-18.

13

The Great Intercessory Prayer

(John 17:1-21)

IVAN FRENCH

This is indeed one of the holy places of Scripture. We won't tarry here long, not because there isn't much for us to ponder but maybe because there is too much. Whole books have been written on these words of our Lord. Over a century ago, Marcus Rainsford wrote nearly five hundred pages of very careful exposition of this prayer of the Lord Jesus. This is the prayer He prayed in the presence of His disciples on the night before He died. It follows the Upper Room Discourse in chapters 14, 15, and 16 of John's Gospel. Now, I'm quite sure they left that room and went down the eastern slope of the little mountain upon which the city of Jerusalem is built. They crossed the little level area they call the Valley of Kidron and probably began the ascent of the Mount of Olives, the lower level of which is the Garden of Gethsemane.

This is not the Gethsemane prayer. That comes just a little bit later, as Jesus withdrew from His apostles and went into the solitude of that quiet place. This was prayed in the presence of His apostles. It is of great value to us because it is rich in practical and doctrinal truth. Indeed, who can fathom the mystery of God the Son in prayer to God the Father? It affords us a glimpse of our Lord's ministry in heaven today as our great High Priest, because we are told plainly in Hebrews 7:25 that He lives ever to "make intercession" for us. In that and other passages that speak of His present-day ministry, we are simply told that He intercedes, but we are not given any content. It just may be as the believer ponders carefully the truth that is here in John 17, he will get at least in suggestion form a hint of that for which our Savior prays today.

It may be that we also have here a fitting model for our own praying. I recognize that the Lord has given us a pattern for our prayer elsewhere in that disciple's prayer that begins, "Our Father who is in heaven." But at least it is valuable to observe here that our Lord first of all prays for Himself (17:1-5); then He prays for His immediate apostles, those men who are going out in a special way to represent Him and preach His message. That's verses 6-19. Then, beginning at verse 20, He prays for His church, as He looks down through the ages even to this present hour. And so, it seems to me, when we as believers go to our prayer closets morning by morning, it is completely fitting to first of all pray for ourselves. In praying for yourself, you prepare your heart for that intercessory work that you do. In praying for yourself, there is that confession of sin and that thanksgiving to God and that due worship. Then, you wonder what to pray for? Oh, pray for the servants of the Lord you know, the pastors and the missionaries who are laboring in various parts of the world, and then the vistas of your prayer will be as wide as the church of Christ itself, whether in America or Asia or Africa or South America. Pray for the church, the people of the church, those you may know personally and intimately and those of whom you can only say as Paul said on at least four different occasions, "I make mention of you in my prayers." There is an expansion of the object of praying that is suggested in this prayer: first, Jesus prayed for Himself, then for His apostles, and then for the entire church. And it is to these three areas of prayer that I want us to look for just a little bit.

Jesus Prayed for Himself (John 17:1-5)

> [1] *Jesus spoke these things; and lifting up His eyes to heaven, He said, "Father, the hour has come; glorify Your Son, that the Son may glorify You, [2] even as You gave Him authority over all flesh, that to all whom You have given Him, He may give eternal life. [3] This is eternal life, that they may know You, the only true God, and Jesus Christ whom You have sent. [4] I glorified You on the earth, having accomplished the work*

which You have given Me to do. ⁵ *Now, Father, glorify*
Me together with Yourself, with the glory which I had
with You before the world was."

First of all, Jesus prayed for Himself. If we were to look for a word that would characterize what He has to say here, it would be the word *glorification* because He prays, "Glorify Your Son, that the Son may glorify You." In verse 5 He says, "Now, Father, glorify Me together with Yourself, with the glory which I had with You." And even as we try to think for a minute about that, I recognize that this word *glory* is one of the most difficult in all of Scripture to define because there are so many different uses. However, we cannot look at this little paragraph for very long without realizing that here Jesus was considering the cross and the work He would do there to be His glory. He was praying that His Father would now bring Him to the completion of that work of the cross toward which He was heading. Therefore, we do well to ask this question: In what sense would the cross, with all of its ugliness and its pain and its suffering, be the glory of Christ?

Number one, it would mark the completion of His work. That work upon the cross, maybe just twelve hours away at this point, was the consummation of all He came into the world to do. "You shall call His name Jesus," said the angel to Joseph, "for He will save His people from their sins." He would save us by His death as our substitute upon the cross, so He steadfastly set His face to go to Jerusalem. He let nothing turn Him aside from that task, and tomorrow would mark the completion of the work He came to do.

But that same work would glorify the Father in heaven because it would demonstrate a perfect obedience on the part of the Son to the Father. He became "obedient unto death, even the death of the cross" (Phil. 2:8). We honor that one whom we obey. Children, you do not honor your parents when you disobey them. You disgrace them, and you dishonor them. We do not honor our employer or that one who is our superior when we disobey them. We honor them and we show our respect when we obey them. Jesus obeyed to the very last breath of His life the will of His heavenly Father for the salvation of man.

But I notice also in this little section that He makes a request to return to His preincarnate glory, that is, the glory He had before He came to earth: "Now, Father, glorify Me together with Yourself, with the glory which I had with You before the world was." We get just a little glimpse of that in the sixth chapter of the book of Isaiah: "In the year of King Uzziah's death I saw the Lord sitting on a throne, lofty and exalted, with the train of His robe filling the temple. Seraphim stood above Him" (Isa. 6:1-2). We know so little about these seraphim, but they seem to be those guardians of the throne of God, those angelic beings always associated with the holiness of God. One cried to another saying, "Holy, Holy, Holy, is the Lord of hosts, the whole earth is full of His glory" (v. 3). So effective was that chant that we read that the very doorposts of the heavenly temple shook, and the house was filled with smoke (v. 4). It's a picture of divine majesty. It's a picture of universal dominion.

And in John 12:41, we discover that the One who was sitting upon that throne was none other than Jesus Christ in His preincarnate glory. He left that place of the universal dominion, where He was the object of the worship and adoration of the highest created intelligence. He came down, down, down into this dirty and difficult world in order to mount a cross, there to pay for your sins and mine.

But in John 17 Jesus is getting homesick. I think we have seen it before as time after time He slipped away from the busy activities of these ministries to spend the night on a nearby mountain and there pray to His heavenly Father. Now He expresses it in this prayer: "Glorify Me … with the glory which I had with You before the world was" (v. 5). And all of that was connected with the cross, because He recognized that the cross was the beginning of the way home, as He moved through crucifixion and resurrection and ascension and exaltation, and finally sat down at the right hand of the throne of God, where He is today. Jesus was saying, "I'm homesick. Let us get the work done so I can get back home."

Jesus Prayed for His Apostles (John 17:6-19)

[6] *"I have manifested Your name to the men whom You gave Me out of the world; they were Yours and You gave them to Me, and they have kept Your word. [7] Now they have come to know that everything You have given Me is from You; [8] for the words which You gave Me I have given to them; and they received them and truly understood that I came forth from You, and they believed that You sent Me. [9] I ask on their behalf; I do not ask on behalf of the world, but of those whom You have given Me; for they are Yours; [10] and all things that are Mine are Yours, and Yours are Mine ; and I have been glorified in them. [11] I am no longer in the world; and yet they themselves are in the world, and I come to You. Holy Father, keep them in Your name, the name which You have given Me, that they may be one even as We are. [12] While I was with them, I was keeping them in Your name which You have given Me; and I guarded them and not one of them perished but the son of perdition, so that the Scripture would be fulfilled.*

[13] *"But now I come to You; and these things I speak in the world so that they may have My joy made full in themselves. [14] I have given them Your word; and the world has hated them, because they are not of the world, even as I am not of the world. [15] I do not ask You to take them out of the world, but to keep them from the evil one. [16] They are not of the world, even as I am not of the world. [17] Sanctify them in the truth; Your word is truth. [18] As You sent Me into the world, I also have sent them into the world. [19] For their sakes I sanctify Myself, that they themselves also may be sanctified in truth."*

But Jesus not only prayed for Himself; He prayed also for His apostles. That is what we have here in verses 6 through 19. It is clear in verse 9 who He has in mind: "I pray for them: I pray not for the world, but for them which thou hast given me; for they are thine" (KJV). Not now for the world, did He pray, but for His servants who would go out to reach the world. It is rather interesting to observe that Jesus, as far as the record is concerned, never prayed for individual lost people. He prayed for those whom He would send out to reach the lost—those preachers and teachers and witnesses to His truth—and that is what He is doing here. We have a delightful little pattern here for those times when we don't know exactly what to pray for. Look at the four things Jesus prayed for here.

First, He asks in verse 11 that His Father will "keep them": "I am no longer in the world; and *yet* they themselves are in the world, and I come to You. Holy Father, keep them in Your name." The word He uses here has the idea of guarding or protecting, but isn't it interesting that it does not say *what* He is to keep them from. He's going to use the same word later on but with specific reference. The disciples demonstrated they were prone to dissension, to difficulty, and to discord. They were always fussing with one another, displaying those old carnal natures, each of them saying, "I want to be at the head of the line." Could it be the Lord is praying, "Father, keep them from coming apart, keep them from having those disagreements with one another, from that dissent, that division, that discord that tends to hurt their ministries"? You remember when Mrs. Zebedee came, interceding for her two sons. We have reason to suspect that the two sons put her up to it, but she came to Jesus and said she wanted James and John to sit on one side and the other of Jesus in His kingdom. That was a very substantial request, I would say. Jesus had a few words in response. Read the account in Matthew 20, and you will discover that when the other apostles heard the request James and John had made, they were—well the KJV uses this lovely, dignified word—*indignant.* It means they were mad. They didn't like it. There was discord, there was dissension, and through all these last six months of the life of our Lord, He was dealing with the apostles, trying to teach them something of self-denial, preferring one another, and encouraging one another; but clear down to this very night, just a few hours earlier when they were sitting around the table, where they observed the Passover and where our communion service was established, they were still arguing about which one of them was going to be the greatest in the kingdom of God (Luke 22:24). And now as Jesus intercedes for these self-seeking men, He says, "Guard them from this sort of thing."

Do you know that among the servants of the Lord, whether they are at home or on the mission field, the whole matter of inter-personal relationships—specifically, the failure to get along with other people—is the largest single cause of failure in the work of God? Many missionaries have had to come home from the mission field after one term or before one term was even over because they could not get along with their coworkers. When you pray for the servants of the Lord, whether they are pastors, evangelists, or mis-sionaries, pray that God will keep them from that ugly expression of selfish hearts that so often causes discord. Pray that God will teach us all how to give and take, and be pliable, and defer to others with whom we may not quite see eye to eye. Jesus prayed, "Keep them."

And then He says in verse 13, "Give them joy." His exact words are, "These things I speak in the world, that they might have my joy fulfilled in themselves" (KJV). Now this is an intensely interesting thing, because Jesus is sending these men into a difficult and dan-gerous world. All but one of them is probably going to lay down his life in a violent death. There is going to be all kinds of heartache and privation and loss along the way, and yet He has already said, "These things I have spoken to you so that My joy may be in you, and *that* your joy may be made full" (John 15:11). It is one of the glorious things of the Christian life that there is a joy possessed by the child of God who dwells in the Scripture. There is a joy that is able to rise above and shine through the difficulties, the dis-appointments, the heartaches, the hurts, the dangers, of this pres-ent life. As He was about to send these fellows out into this difficult assignment, He prayed, "Lord, give them joy in everything they do."

Then he says something else, and here is that expression again in verse 15: "keep them." The request is preceded by Jesus' statement, "I do not ask You to take them out of the world." It's rather interesting that there are times in the pressure of things, when many of God's people say to the Lord, "How long? Let's wind this up. Let's pray for the rapture." Sometimes we even long for death. As long as we are here in the world, the Lord of life and death is in control of things, and He says concerning these men, "I do not ask You to take them out of the world, but to keep them from the evil one." "Evil" is a word in the masculine gender, which means He is talking about a person—the evil *one*. The evil one is Satan. Thus, He is praying, "Keep Your servants from the onslaughts of Satan."

The devil hates God with a passion, and he hates all of God's people. As long as the devil is alive and working in the world, he will seek to deceive the servants of Christ, damage their devotion, and even bring them to the point of premature death. And sometimes God for mysterious reasons allows him to do that (cf. Heb. 2:14). Here Jesus prays that the Father will bolster and embolden these men against the onslaughts of Satan. That means we, like them, need to know a little something about what the apostle Paul calls the "schemes," or wiles, the methods, of the devil. We need to put on the armor of God by which we can resist him, and Jesus is praying, "Lord, protect your servants."

And then there is one other thing in verse 17: "Sanctify them in the truth." If I were looking for words to characterize this prayer, I think I would choose two. The first would be *preservation*: "keep them." The second would be *sanctification*. Here is another one of those biblical words about which we need to pause and ask what it means. *To sanctify* means *to set apart*, and setting something apart makes it different. When the utensils that were to be used in the tabernacle were sanctified (Exod. 30:26-29), they were set apart; they were going to be used for a different purpose than the other knives and forks and pots and pans. When the garments the priests wore were sanctified (Exod. 28:2), they were set apart for one holy purpose, and that was to be worn by the priests when they went into the service of the Lord.

But now Jesus is talking about His men. He is saying, "Lord, sanctify them; set them apart." We know from the New Testament teaching that there is a positional sanctification. We are set apart in our position. By virtue of having put our trust in Christ, we are placed in Christ. That is a marvelous thing. And from the moment we trust Him as our Savior, God the Father sees us as being in His Son, set apart, identified with Jesus Christ. Then there is that practical sanctification, that progressive growth as we advance in righteousness and holiness as the truth of God has an increasing grip on our lives. However, there is also a particular sanctification that I believe is in view here. What I mean by particular sanctification is that God sets aside people for a particular task, dedicating them to a specific service. These men were to be set apart by the Word of God. "Sanctify them in the truth; Your word is truth," Jesus said.

May I suggest that there are two very important ideas here. First, they were to be set apart, to be cleansed, *by the Word of God*. "Wherewithal shall a young man cleanse his way? by taking heed thereto according to thy word" (Ps. 119:9 KJV). The Word is the laver to which we go. That is why, dear friends, you must read the Word of God every day. In all kindness I say, if you do not set some time apart to bathe in the Word of God, you will fail in your Christian life. This is the means by which God has ordained that we should be cleansed. So Jesus prays, "Let these men be clean through the Word of God."

But there is something else here. Their ministry is to be a ministry of the Word of God. This is where particular sanctification comes in. Their ministry is to be distinctively a ministry of the Word. They are to be men who are identified as men of the Word. They are to be men who will commit themselves to the teaching and preaching of the Word of God. If I had a whole roomful of my preacher brethren, I think I would spend a couple of hours examining the subtle variations on this particular truth. You know there are movements among us that are drawing those who are called to preach the Word of God away from this main ministry, which is a full-time task. Those who are experts in church growth say you must do this and you must do that. Others say you've got to involve yourself in the community so folks will know where you are. The psychologists and the counselors come along and say you must do this and you must do that. Maybe all of those things have their place, but the ministry of the Word of God is a specialized, full-time ministry, and so many good men of God have been enticed to turn aside to lesser things. Jesus prayed for His own that night, "Sanctify them in [or by] the truth." This was His prayer: "Keep them clean through the Word, and keep them dedicated, committed, pressing on in just one all-consuming life labor and ministry of the Word of God." It's a full-time ministry. You can't do it on a part-time basis. "Sanctify them."

Isn't it interesting that Jesus Himself is the pattern for that sort of thing? Did you catch it in verse 19? "For their sakes I sanctify Myself." That's why I say that progressive sanctification is not the principal truth here, though it's certainly an important one. Jesus did not need to grow in holiness. He was the sinless one. But He was saying, "I have devoted myself to one task." Here He steadfastly set His face to Jerusalem. He had said earlier, "My food is to do the will of Him who sent Me and to accomplish His work" (John 4:34). He has already prayed that God would allow Him to glorify His Father through an absolute obedience. Now He is saying, "I'm the example of what I mean by being set apart to one particular task and labor. I am going to the cross tomorrow. And on that cross the moment will come when I will say, 'It is finished.' And I will have accomplished that for which I came into the world."

Jesus Prayed for His Church (John 17:20-26)

> [20] "I do not ask on behalf of these alone, but for those also who believe in Me through their word; [21] that they may all be one; even as You, Father, are in Me and I in You, that they also may be in Us, so that the world may believe that You sent Me. [22] The glory which You have given Me I have given to them, that they may be one, just as We are one; [23] I in them and You in Me, that they may be perfected in unity, so that the world may know that You sent Me, and loved them, even as You have loved Me. [24] Father, I desire that they also, whom You have given Me, be

with Me where I am, so that they may see My glory which You have given Me, for You loved Me before the foundation of the world. ²⁵ O righteous Father, although the world has not known You, yet I have known You; and these have known that You sent Me; ²⁶ and I have made Your name known to them, and will make it known, so that the love with which You loved Me may be in them, and I in them."

Finally, beginning in verse 20, Jesus prayed for His church throughout this whole age. Isn't that interesting? He does not pray for the apostles alone but also for those who will believe in Him through their word. The apostles and those who were associated with them wrote the Word down. We have it today. Perhaps you came to Christ because you heard those gracious words, "Come to me ... and I will give you rest" (Matt. 11:28). Those words came from an apostle whose name was Matthew. He listened to Jesus and then wrote down His words. You might have been saved through the gospel in a nutshell, John 3:16: "For God so loved the world, that He gave His only begotten Son, that whoever believes in Him shall not perish, but have eternal life." That is the word of an apostle. Jesus said it, but John wrote it down. Every one of us who is saved has been saved through the word of one of those who was there that night.

If I would, again, try to come up with one word that somehow describes this particular prayer of Jesus, I would use the word *unification.* For Himself He prayed for *glorification;* for His apostles, He prayed for *preservation* and for their *sanctification;* and now as He looks down and reaches out, as it were, to encompass the whole church of every age, He prays for its *unification.*

We come now to what, for me, is one of the most difficult passages, not only in the Gospels, but in all of the New Testament. Here it is: "I do not ask on behalf of these alone, but for those also who believe in Me through their word; that they may all be one." Let me pause here to say that there is a sense in which that prayer has been answered. No matter what outward name we may bear—whether we are Baptist or Methodist or Presbyterian or Brethren or independent—if we are saved, we have the same life of Christ. We are one in Christ. That much is no problem.

However, Jesus prays "that they may all be one; even as You, Father are in Me and I in You, that they also may be in Us, so that the world may believe that You sent Me." And there's the sticker! Jesus is praying here and in verses 22-23 that His people will have an outward manifestation of oneness of some sort, so that the world will see, and through this amazing spiritual unity, displayed by our unity of purpose, unity of thought, unity of devotion—by that unity—people in the world will come to believe. What is the condition of things today? There are more "ics" and "tics" and "isms" and schisms within the church of Christ than you can shake a stick at. Poor John Doe, out here on the street, lost and with a hungry heart and not really knowing what he is searching for, some-how has a sense that in the church there ought to be some answers. But he says, "I looked at this church and this church and this church, and they are all disagreeing and fussing with one another. They are divided over this and divided over that," and he goes on his way very likely to a lost eternity. This prayer of Jesus, as far as I can tell, has not yet been answered.

But consider this for encouragement. His request for Himself was answered. The next day He completed His work upon the cross, and before long He went back to the glory He had with the Father before the world was. His prayer for the apostles was answered. For those men, bound together in a common purpose after the Day of Pentecost and empowered by the Holy Spirit, went out; and in the very words of their critics, these men turned the world upside down. We do not know of one of them who fell by the wayside because of uncleanness, or impurity, or heresy, or anything of that kind. They were kept. They were sanctified in every sense of the word.

If the first part of Jesus' prayer was answered, and if the second part of the prayer was answered, we may be sure that this last part of the prayer also will be answered. How and when, I can only make a suggestion. In 2 Thessalonians 1 we have a graphic description of the return of Jesus Christ with His people. One of these days we're going to hear the voice of the archangel and the trump of God. I do not know when we will be caught up, but the whole church will be caught up to be with Him (1 Thess. 4:16-17). There will be a time of judgment and cleansing, not judgment for salvation but for reward at the judgment seat of Christ (2 Cor. 5:10). There will be a joining together—can I use the word *officially*—with Jesus Christ and with all the rest of the members of the body described in Revelation 19 at the marriage supper of the Lamb. Down here on earth, political and military things will be coming to a head in that great conflict we call the battle of Armageddon, when kings of the earth gather together against the Lord and against His Christ. In the midst of the crisis of that coming day, we read this: "For after all it is *only* just for God to repay with affliction those who afflict you, and *to give* relief to you who are afflicted and to us as well when the Lord Jesus will be revealed from heaven with His mighty angels in flaming fire, dealing out retribution to those who do not know God and to those who do not obey the gospel of our Lord Jesus" (2 Thess. 1:6-8). Verse 10 tells us He comes in that day "to be glorified." How? "In His saints." If I understand that passage correctly, it is saying something like this: On that day when His great work of perfection and glorification of His church is complete, He will come back with His church as His body and His bride, and then the world will see that they are one. There will be a unification, a unity, that the whole world at that time will see.

Consider this: It is rather amazing to read in 2 Corinthians 13:4 that Christ died in weakness. "For though He was crucified in weakness, yet He lives by the power of God" (NKJV). He was raised in power. The apostles ministered in weaknesses. Paul wrote, "God has chosen the weak things of the world to shame the things which are strong" (1 Cor. 1:27). You can't find a better description of that group of apostles than in that paragraph (vv. 26-28). They were weak, but through the indwelling Holy Spirit, their labors were mighty and powerful. And we know that every individual Christian also is weak; yet we are strong as we lean upon Him.

I can't put my finger on any single verse of Scripture to demonstrate exactly what I want to say here, but it may well be that God is allowing the church, the institutional church, the church that everyone can see, whatever name you want to give to it, with all its divisions and all its dissension, to demonstrate how utterly weak we are. With all of our flaunted organization, with all of our adoption of the world's methods, and all too often the world's values and the world's thought patterns, one of these days, having failed to demonstrate this unity for which Jesus prayed, we are going to be caught up, purified, and joined to Jesus Christ. Then by a mighty act of power, when Jesus comes back again, we will be with Him, and we will be the objects of the gaze of the world; and they will glorify Christ because of us. They will say, "Jesus Christ is wonderful after all. Look at what He did with that bunch of stubborn, rebellious sinners. Down here they were always dividing and splitting and fussing, majoring on the minors and minoring on the majors, and all the rest." And the prayer of John 17:21 and 23 will be answered.

One more word, and then I'm through. God spoke to my heart through verse 24 many years ago. It is a wonderful thing. Remember now, this is our Lord praying to God the Father. This is His request: "Father, I desire that they also, whom You have given Me, be with Me where I am, so that they may see My glory." He is praying here for us—for you and me. If I were to ask, "Do you want to go to heaven? Do you want to be with the Lord Jesus?" every truly born-again heart would say, yes, indeed. But there is something surpassingly amazing about the fact that Jesus wants us there with Him far more than we want to be there! "Father, I desire that they also, whom You have given Me, be with Me where I am."

Some call the church in its visible form on the earth the *church militant*. I don't know how militant it is sometimes, but that title is used in contrast with the saved people who have already gone to heaven, who are called the *church triumphant*. Well, recognizing those terms for whatever they are worth, what is happening is something like this: In this age one by one God is taking His own to join the church triumphant. Every time a Christian dies, the prayer of John 17:24 is being answered. One by one the people of God are going to where He is, that they might behold His glory. When that number is complete, the church militant on earth will be caught up in what we call the rapture. It will be purified, protected, and perfected, and it will return with our Lord Jesus. May I give you another word? I would like to call that the *church evident*. Finally, it will be evident to everybody that the church is one, that the church is a unity. That which we have failed to do as a church in this dispensation will be done by the mighty power of God. The church militant will be taken up to become the church triumphant and sent back to be the church evident. Even in thinking about that, the hearts of many will cry out, "Lord, hasten the day."

Conclusion

In this great prayer of Jesus, He refers to His own apostles or the church as those "whom You have given Me." Do you remember that wonderful word in John 6:37: "All that the Father gives Me will come to Me, and the one who comes to Me I will certainly not cast out"? That church for whom Jesus prayed is made up of those whom God the Father has given to God the Son, and they have made that manifest, evident, by the fact that they've come to Jesus Christ in faith, believing. Have you come to Christ today? Will you place your faith in Jesus and become part of that grand body for whom Jesus prayed, "I desire that they ... be with Me where I am, so that they may see My glory"?

Four Miracles at the Cross

ROBERT B. LANNING

Matthew mentions four miracles in his account of the crucifixion of Christ, and each is worthy of our consideration and reflection.

The first miracle was the darkness that fell upon "all the land" at noon and continued for the last three hours of Jesus' crucifixion (Matt. 27:45). That darkness was not the result of natural phenomena like a solar eclipse. Jesus' crucifixion happened near the time of the Jewish Passover, which occurs when the moon is full, and a solar eclipse is impossible during the full moon; and no natural eclipse would have lasted for three hours anyway. The darkness was not the result of a thunderstorm or sandstorm, because neither is mentioned in the Scriptures and Luke states that the sun itself ceased, or failed (Luke 23:45, Greek *ekleipō*). This darkness was a supernatural miracle from the hand of God, similar to the one He performed through Moses in Egypt, when He sent "a darkness which may be felt" over all the land for three days, even though the Jews had light in their dwellings during that time (Exod. 10: 21-23). Beginning at the time of the sun's zenith, this sudden darkness must have been quite startling to everyone assembled at Calvary. The fact that it ceased at the moment of Christ's death, apparently just as suddenly as when it appeared, must have made it even more amazing.

The significance of this miracle may be that it demonstrated in a dramatic way God's judgment against Christ for all mankind's sins, since darkness in the Scriptures is often associated with God's supernatural judgments against men (see Joel 2:30-31; Amos 5:18-20; Zeph. 1:14-16; Matt. 24:29; Rev. 6:12). It also may have been planned by God to shield Jesus from being clearly seen by others at Calvary as He experienced the full measure of God's wrath. And perhaps it also showed that nature itself sympathized with Christ as He endured such an agonizing death.

The second miracle at Calvary was the rending of the temple veil that separated the Holy of Holies from the Holy Place. This happened at the moment of Christ's death and is introduced by Matthew with the phrase "And behold" (Matt. 27:51), showing his sense of wonder at its occurrence. This massive curtain, some sixty feet long and twenty feet wide, with a thickness of four inches, was "torn in two from top to bottom," indicating that God, not man, had done it. Matthew mentions this event before the earthquake, so its occurrence was not likely due to that phenomenon.

The tearing of the temple veil signified God's termination of the Jewish priesthood and its prescribed temple rituals. The author of Hebrews states that the veil represented Jesus' flesh, which was "torn" at Calvary, opening for believers a new and living way of access into the presence of God (Heb. 10:19-22). He now is our great High Priest (Heb. 4:14) who "always lives to make intercession" for us (Heb. 7:25). This miracle may well have had a significant effect on Israel's priests, a great many of whom soon thereafter became obedient to the Christian faith (Acts 6:7)

The third miracle at Calvary, one mentioned only by Matthew, was that "the earth shook and the rocks were split" (Matt. 27:51), causing the tombs to open (v. 52). This must have been a powerful earthquake; for it shook the earth so strongly that the rocks were split into pieces, and the tombs in the rocks sprang open. God's awesome control over nature was evident in this earthquake, just as it had been in the earthquake He sent on Mount Sinai at the giving of the Mosaic law (Exod. 19:18). The reaction of the centurion and his detachment of soldiers at the cross upon seeing "the earthquake and the things that were happening" was one of extreme fear. Yet the earthquake, at least in part, also evoked their faith, for they said, "Truly this was the Son of God!" (Matt. 27:54).

The fourth and final miracle, also mentioned only in Matthew's account of the crucifixion, was that "many bodies of the saints who had fallen asleep were raised; and coming out of the tombs after His resurrection they entered into the holy city and appeared to many" (Matt. 27:52-53). This resurrection was granted only to dead believers ("saints"), not to the general cemetery population of

Jerusalem. Although there is a wide range of opinion about when this happened, it seems that Matthew is stating that it happened after Jesus' resurrection. In support of this view, it should be recalled that Paul declared before Herod Agrippa II at Caesarea that Christ "should suffer, and that he should be the first that should rise from the dead" (Acts 26:23 KJV). Later in 1 Corinthians he stated that the resurrected Christ is "the first fruits of those who are asleep" (1 Cor. 15:20). Six other believers mentioned in both the Old and New Testaments had been resuscitated from death, only to die again, but Christ led the way in being the first person ever to receive an incorruptible, eternal resurrection body. His resurrection is a pledge that we too will receive such a glorious resurrection body from the gracious hand of God (John 14:19; 2 Cor. 4:14; Phil. 3:20-21).

Although we have no detailed word in the Scriptures about what happened to these saints who were raised after they appeared to many in Jerusalem, it is possible, if they received resurrection bodies, that they were later taken to heaven with Christ around the time of His ascension (Eph. 4:8-10).

14

The One Foolproof Evidence

(Matthew 28:1-15)

ERNIE GODSHALL

If you are a Christian, you believe in the literal, physical, bodily resurrection of Christ. So I don't want to carry ice cubes to Eskimos in this message. But I wonder, do you really grasp its significance? Do you realize what this says about every other world religion? It means Christianity is true and all the others are false. Neither Islam nor Judaism nor any other religion has a risen Savior. Do you know what Christ's resurrection says about the future? Jesus Christ is Lord of both the living and the dead.

Do you realize that the same power that raised Christ from the dead is at work in every believer? Do you live in the truth that Christ's resurrection power is the source of all your growing and changing and victory over sin? Your growth in godliness, your bearing fruit for God, your sanctification, your putting off sin and putting on godliness—all are driven and empowered by Christ's resurrection (Romans 6–8; Ephesians 1–2).

Do you realize that this message of Christ risen from the dead is what fired up and fueled all the preaching in the book of Acts? The apostles' bold message was basically this: "You murdered Him, but God raised Him up, so repent and believe in Him!" Do you realize how the resurrection of Christ is God's declaration that His work on the cross has been accepted and that the war has been won?

Do you realize Christ has taken the sting out of death, and for His people "to be absent from the body" is "to be present with the Lord" (2 Cor. 5:8)? And do you see that Christ's resurrection is the reason we do not grieve as others do in the face of the death of our loved ones (1 Thess. 4:14)?

Christ is all we need. We are justified by faith in Him alone. He is the Lamb standing in heaven as if slain, alive forever to intercede and represent us at God's right hand. Do you fully realize that the resurrection is the one, foolproof evidence that our faith is not in vain, that Christianity is true—that we will not be disappointed? And do you understand that faith in Christ's resurrection is required to be saved (Rom. 10:9-10)?

Let's go to Matthew 28 and follow the story as it unfolds. After Christ's death and burial, the Jewish leaders were concerned about the disciples stealing the body. They were thinking, "No way are we letting those deluded disciples get in there and steal the body of that blasphemer!" So Pilate gave permission for the stone covering the tomb's entrance to be sealed and a guard to be put in place. The stone may have weighed a ton. The seal was probably a cord stretched across the stone sealed at each end with wax, and, according to Barnes, up to sixty soldiers may have been appointed to guard the tomb, possibly divided into watches through the night.[1] So we pick up the account in Matthew 28.

A World-Shaking Experience (Matt. 28:1-5)

> [1] *Now after the Sabbath, as it began to dawn toward the first day of the week, Mary Magdalene and the other Mary came to look at the grave.* [2] *And behold, a severe earthquake had occurred, for an angel of the Lord descended from heaven and came and rolled away the stone and sat upon it.* [3] *And his appearance was like lightning, and his clothing as white as snow.* [4] *The guards shook for fear of him and became like dead men.* [5] *The angel said to the women, "Do not be afraid; for I know that you are looking for Jesus who has been crucified."*

---

[1] Albert Barnes, *Barnes' Notes on the New Testament* (Grand Rapids: Kregel, 1962), 144.

There are very few experiences that totally change everything. The next few moments would change the world, not only for these ladies but also for all people for all time. They came "to look at the grave" (Matt. 28:1). We know from the other Gospels they brought perfume and spices to anoint Jesus' body (cf. Mark 16:1; Luke 23:55–24:1). They came in deepest grief, severe disappointment, and loyal love. They didn't come expecting anything but His cold, dead body.

God had sent an angel clothed in lightning, electrifyingly brilliant, to greet these ladies. Yes, there were two angels (cf. Luke 24:4-5), but Matthew focuses on this one (Matt. 28:2-3). Let's look at the power of God here. A "severe" *(mega)* earthquake *(seismos)* accompanied the angel who rolled the stone away before the ladies arrived, and now he was sitting on the stone. He was not standing there but sitting there, on top of the stone. I just like that. When do you sit down? After the work is done! Perhaps he was thinking, "I have this huge privilege in all the great events, all the world-shaking, history-changing moments, to sit here giving witness to the resurrection." There he was sitting on this stone he himself had rolled away—not so Jesus could get out but so the women (and we) could look in. He was sitting there symbolizing Christ's victory, as if saying, "We won! The Victor has emerged, and the Warrior has conquered. Hope has dawned bright for a dying humanity. The cosmic war is strategically won. Sin and death and the devil have been smashed. The future is secure."

This lightning-clad, heavenly messenger scared these guards senseless! When Matthew says they "shook for fear of him" (v. 4), he uses *seiō,* the verb form of the word for earthquake (v. 2). They experienced an earthquake in their inner beings! And boom! They fell over unconscious! There were dead-like Roman guards lying all around! This was much like when that large contingent came to arrest Jesus in the garden. When Jesus asked them, "Whom do you seek?" they answered "Jesus." Jesus replied, "I am." And boom! Down they went (John 18:3-6)! How easily God can crush His enemies, yet how patient He is with unbelievers. All three—the stone, the seal, and the guard—were totally powerless before the Lord.

This scheme to keep Jesus' body in the grave was as fruitless as trying to ward off that recent tsunami that swept over the east coast of Japan with a Lego barricade, or like trying to extinguish the sun with a water pistol. How futile are man's efforts to deny God and Christ and the Word of God. God smashes right through it all.

But now, these dear, precious ladies, God bless them, these devotees of Jesus, were shaking with fear, astounded. These were life-changing, world-changing, history-changing moments. They would never be the same. This God-sent, glorious messenger embraced them with his words. One commentator says, "Let us learn that all God's angels are our lovers and helpers, if we love and seek Jesus."[2] The angel told the women, "Do not be afraid." In essence, he said, "I know why you've come. You saw your Lord crucified. You love Him so much, and you are seeking Him. But you are seeking Him as if He were still dead."

Now, listen up: better news no human ears have ever heard. The resurrection is what sets Christianity apart from all other faiths and assures us that Christ is who He said He is and did what He said He'd do.

A World-Changing Message (Matt. 28:6-7)

> [6] *"He is not here, for He has risen, just as He said. Come, see the place where He was lying.* [7] *Go quickly and tell His disciples that He has risen from the dead; and behold, He is going ahead of you into Galilee, there you will see Him; behold, I have told you."*

Here is a five-point message that takes ten seconds to preach. I want to engraft these five points into our hearts this day. Before we look at them, though, imagine if the atheist Richard Dawkins were right. In a debate he said, "We come down to the resurrection of Jesus. It's so petty. It's so trivial. It's so local. It's so earthbound." If he were right, we can imagine the five points would look like this:

---

[2] Alexander Maclaren, *Expositions of Holy Scripture, St. Matthew* (reprint, Whitefish, MT: Kessinger, n.d.), 497.

#1 He's still here, ladies.

#2 He's not risen.

#3 He said He would, but it didn't happen.

#4 Come and see. His body is still there.

#5 Go, tell His disciples He's dead. Their hopes are smashed forever. The enterprise has failed.

It's almost unbearable to even say this, isn't it? If His body were still in that tomb, it would mean the permanent triumph of wrong over right, evil over good, death over life, and it would mean Satan was victorious over God. But what did the angel say? Take this into your minds and hearts, and savor every point.

#1 He's not here!

Oh, let these words reverberate around the world! Proclaim them near and far! How can it be that some schools right here in America aren't allowed to celebrate Easter anymore? How can it be? Let's shout it out like the angel: "He's not here! Ladies, you came to look at the grave, to anoint His body. You expected Him to be here, but He's not here!"

#2 He is risen!

"He was dead; you saw Him. But now He is risen. He's alive, breathing, walking, and warm. His mind is active. His hands and feet and side still carry the scars; you'll see them. This isn't a myth or legend or cover-up to make us all look good. No, God sent me. I'm sitting on this stone throne that used to cover that tomb right there to prove to you forever that He is risen. This is the one final, foolproof evidence that your faith is not in vain. He is risen." This was the angel's glorious revelation.

#3 Just as He said

This was the angel's reminder that Jesus had told them about this many times during the previous three years. They were caught up in total amazement every step of the way, but when He talked about His coming death, they missed His assurance that He would rise again. Jesus told His disciples, "The Son of Man is going to be delivered into the hands of men; and they will kill Him, and He will be raised on the third day" (Matt.17:22-23). But they were "deeply grieved." It's as if they never heard those last nine words: "and He will be raised on the third day."

And He did rise from the dead, *just as He said.* And you can write it down, for everything God says, He will do. He keeps His word, always. He told Abraham his offspring would be in slavery four hundred years and then be brought out. Sure enough, down into Egypt they went for four hundred years; and then God sent them Moses, and they followed him to freedom through the Red Sea. He promised them the land flowing with milk and honey, and every one of His promises came true. What incredible words we find in Joshua 21:45: "Not one of the good promises which the LORD had made to the house of Israel failed; all came to pass."

Do you believe this Book? Listen, there is a mind and a sovereign hand behind all sixty-six books of the Bible. God controls everything, from beginning to end. Christ told His followers that He'd die and then rise again. And He did! Just as He said He would. Whatever God says He's going to do, He does. You can believe Him. This world has a built-in bias against believing God, but let's write it down: "God said it. That settles it. I believe it." He said He'd rise again, and He did.

What else did He say? He said He will come again and receive us to Himself, and He will. He said "every knee will bow" before Him, and they will—every one. Every person you know will bow. Every rock star we know will bow—Hendrix, Clapton, Joplin. Every world leader we know will bow—Churchill, LBJ, Kennedy, Reagan, Clinton, and Obama. Every human butcher and mass murderer will bow—Herod, Hitler, Hussein. Every financial wizard will bow—Buffet, Gates, Trump. Every atheist, false teacher, mocker, and hypocrite—Mohammed himself—all will fall on their knees before this risen, living Lord and Judge, "just as He said."

So these ladies came to anoint Jesus' body. Imagine standing there with them and hearing, "He is risen, JUST AS HE SAID!" Wow!

#4 Come and see

What an invitation this was. But God invites all of us: Look around. "Do you see His body, ladies? You were there when Joseph of Arimathea laid His dead, lifeless body in the tomb. You were there and saw Nicodemus, the teacher of Israel, with one hundred pounds of spices to prepare Jesus' body for burial (John 19:38-39). Look, is He there?"

What did the women see? They saw the linen bandages lying here, and over there the face cloth all folded up neatly, majestically, everything in its place. But no body. It was the most wonderful "nobody" you'll ever see. Come, feast your eyes on it! Let it totally consume your heart. He walked out of that death tomb gloriously alive! He is not there. We serve a living, risen, true, unique Lord and Savior. To John in Revelation 1:18 Jesus proclaimed, "I was dead, and behold, I am alive forevermore."

#5 Go quickly and tell!

"Tell His disciples that He has risen from the dead." This is the message we have. He died, and He is risen. This is the final proof, the one foolproof evidence. You can deny it, but you can shut your eyes and deny the sun is out there, too. You can deny it, and go on living as if this life were all there is. You can wrongly say, "Men are born. They live. And they die—that's it." But you'll discover too late how wrong you were. This truth is the keystone of our faith. It is the one final piece that fueled the apostles in the book of Acts, as they preached, "You killed Him, but God raised Him, and now you have one thing to do: repent and believe in Him." Embrace Him by personal faith right now. He is alive and stands at the end of every man and woman's journey. Every one of you will face Him one day.

Jesus' Feet and a Huge Fabrication (Matt. 28:8-15)

> [8] And they left the tomb quickly with fear and great joy and ran to report it to His disciples. [9] And behold, Jesus met them and greeted them. And they came up and took hold of His feet and worshiped Him. [10] Then

Jesus said to them, "Do not be afraid; go and take word to My brethren to leave for Galilee, and there they will see Me."

[11] Now while they were on their way, some of the guard came into the city and reported to the chief priests all that had happened. [12] And when they had assembled with the elders and consulted together, they gave a large sum of money to the soldiers, [13] and said, "You are to say, 'His disciples came by night and stole Him away while we were asleep.' [14] And if this should come to the governor's ears, we will win him over and keep you out of trouble." [15] And they took the money and did as they had been instructed; and this story was widely spread among the Jews, and is to this day.

Would you not be shaking at this point? The women ran, shivering with awed fear, but with hearts fairly bursting with joy. This is our joy too—joy unspeakable and full of glory. These women had life-transforming, hope-giving news to report. So do you and I. We have the one message this world needs to hear, in spite of our secularism and relativism and chaos. People need to hear this today, and we ought to be gripped with fear and great joy, overwhelmed by the reality that Jesus rose from the dead! There's only one hope for this world—the risen, ruling, returning Christ!

Verse 9 is so, so good. They were running like sprinters, heading straight for the city, and suddenly who met them? And what did He say? "Good morning, ladies." His words were just the typical greeting *(chairein)*. Instantly they were on their faces, their hands reaching out, touching His feet. What an amazing detail—they took hold of His feet. They were literal, physical, living, warm feet, feet with nail marks—undeniably Jesus' feet.

What did He tell them in verse 10? "Go tell My brothers!" Not, "Go tell those cowards, those betrayers, those quarrelers." No, Jesus said, "Go and take word to My brethren," or brothers. These words indicate more. "They, like you ladies, are in My family, forever. Sure, they stumbled all over themselves and got it mixed up, but I love them. I loved them from the beginning and will love them to the uttermost, just as I love all who receive Me as their Lord and Savior." Then Jesus gave a command: "Go tell them to meet up with Me in Galilee! I've got an assignment for them."

What does this account tell us about the ladies? Men, where were you early that Sunday morning? Playing video games? Sleeping in? Were you cowering, hiding out, afraid of reprisals from the Jewish rulers? These women proved their loyalty and love for their Savior! And God has used women to this very day to be "up and at 'em," telling the good news. On that eventful morning, it was ladies who came early, even before the sun was up, and saw that lightning-clad messenger and heard those world-shaking, world-changing truths.

The great lie is recorded in verses 11-15. What happened to those guards God apparently had knocked out when the angel appeared (v. 4)? Upon regaining consciousness, some of them went and reported to the big-shot religious leaders who had murdered Jesus three days before. And here we have the biggest cover-up in history. What were the soldiers told to do? The chief priests said, "Here's the narrative you need to repeat whenever asked about it, whenever interviewed by the media. Here's the story, here's the fabricated line, to save your necks and protect our reputation and power. Say His disciples came and stole the body while you slept, and we'll cover your tails for you." So much for truth. The religious leaders of that day didn't care about the truth. They cared only about their own reputations. And this lie has been perpetrated down to this very day.

People can say whatever they want about the resurrection. They can call it a myth, a fabrication, a nice ending to a religious fable. But listen again to that angel: "He is not here for He has risen, just as He said. Come, see the place He was lying. Go quickly and tell His disciples that He has risen from the dead." May God fill us with the joy of this reality, not just for today but for the rest of our lives. And if you have never bowed your knee to Christ, do it now!

The Roman Guard at the Empty Tomb

ROBERT B. LANNING

The Gospel of Matthew has many unique features, but one that is often overlooked is the author's account of the Roman guard at the empty tomb, found in Matthew 27 and 28. This narrative gives us insight into the motives of the Jewish leaders and is an effective apologetic for the historicity of Christ's resurrection.

After his account of Jesus' burial by Joseph of Arimathea (Matt. 27:57-61), Matthew explained that the Jewish chief priests and Pharisees approached Pilate on "the next day, the day after the preparation" (Matt. 27:62). This was the Jewish Sabbath, our Saturday. In contrast to John 18:28 they felt no further need to keep themselves from entering the Praetorium, perhaps because by then the Passover was over. They respectfully addressed Pilate as "Sir" (*kurios* in Greek, Matt. 27:63) but spoke disparagingly of Jesus, calling Him "that deceiver" and thus refusing even to pronounce His name. They told Pilate they remembered that Christ had predicted He would rise again after three days. This comment revealed that they understood Christ's prediction, even though Jesus' closest disciples were still mystified by it (as in John 20:9). Perhaps Jesus' opponents finally had seen the meaning behind Christ's public predictions of His resurrection (in John 2:19 and Matt. 12:40).

Next, they requested that Pilate command that Jesus' grave be made secure until the third day, lest His disciples steal away His body and then claim He had risen from the dead, which in their view would cause even more problems than Jesus' claim to be the Son of God (Matt. 27:64). They were convinced Jesus' claim to deity and His prediction that He would rise from the dead were both deceptions and that His disciples would "manufacture" a false resurrection by stealing His body and then claiming His prediction had come true. This line of reasoning showed they believed the disciples were unscrupulous, dishonest, and desperate men, willing to promote their cause by using underhanded means. It was also a reflection of their own true character, since they had already done the same sort of thing when they gathered false testimony against Jesus at His trial in order to put Him to death (Matt. 26:59-62). It also revealed their sense of powerlessness to prevent such a thing from happening, because the temple police under their command had no legal jurisdiction outside the temple precincts. The Jewish leaders seriously misread the attitude of Jesus' disciples, which was one of dark grief and utter despair (cf. Mark 16:10). They were stunned and saddened by Jesus' death and so much in fear of being apprehended by the Jews that they locked the doors of their meeting place (John 20:19).

Pilate's response was to grant the Jewish leaders their request, giving them a Roman guard and encouraging them to go and secure the tomb "as you know how" (Matt. 27:65). Somewhat surprisingly, Pilate made no attempt to thwart their desires, which was in marked contrast to his recent refusal to change the inscription he had written on Jesus' cross (John 19:19-22). Likely, he saw no point in infuriating the Jews any further, since Jesus was now dead and in the grave.

With their request granted, the leaders traveled to the grave and made it secure (Matt. 27:66). They and the Roman guard together placed a seal on the stone covering the tomb's entrance. Thus the power of the Roman Empire was protecting the tomb of Jesus, and anyone who tampered with its seal would face the wrath of its considerable might. While this must have seemed very satisfying to the Jewish leaders, in reality it proved to be clear evidence that no one ever tampered with the tomb of Christ, since neither friend nor foe would have been able to open the tomb without a battle and likely detection as to their identity.

Matthew also was the only biblical writer to describe the activity of the Roman guard at the time of the descent of the angel from heaven to roll away the stone in front of Jesus' tomb. He recorded that after they saw what had happened, "they shook for fear of him [the angel] and became like dead men" (Matt. 28:4). How powerless their weapons and armor seemed in the awesome presence of the supernatural power of God! They shook for fear for a time and then became still as a stone. It is interesting that the angel made no attempt to speak to them and addressed only the women who came to the tomb (vv. 5-7). How undisturbed the angel was by the presence of these soldiers!

Matthew then recorded that after the women left the tomb area, some (but not all) of the Roman guard made their way into Jerusalem and "reported to the chief priests all that had happened" (Matt. 28:11). The priests must have been flabbergasted to hear the soldiers' account! Here was a witness to the reality of Christ's resurrection from the lips of despised Gentiles! But the depth of the Jewish leaders' depravity is shown by the fact that instead of repenting of their sin of rejecting and crucifying Jesus, they instead gathered with the elders to convene another session of the Sanhedrin (as in Matt. 12:14 and 27:1, 7) to plot out their response to these events. The plan they approved included giving a large amount of money ("much silver" in the Greek) to the soldiers, thus bribing them to spread a false report about what really had happened (Matt. 28:12-13). They were to say, "His disciples came by night and stole Him away while we were asleep." This explanation is easily refuted. If the guards truly had fallen asleep, how would they have known who had stolen the body? Surely they would have awakened at the noise of tomb robbers trying to roll the heavy stone away, and some sort of scuffle would have ensued. They could have pursued and overtaken the thieves, who could not quickly carry a lifeless body to another location.

Finally, the Jewish leaders promised to protect the soldiers from Pilate's wrath if he discovered Jesus' body had been taken from the tomb. For a soldier to be derelict in his duty was punishable by death, as happened soon afterward when Herod put to death the soldiers who had not been able to prevent Peter's supernatural release from prison the night before he was to be put to death (Acts 12:6-7, 18-19). The spokesman for the Sanhedrin told the guards, "We will win him [Pilate] over and keep you out of trouble" (Matt. 28:14). Their persuasion of Pilate, if necessary, probably took the form of another bribe, which again shows their despicable character.

The reaction of the soldiers was predictable: "They took the money and did as they had been instructed" (Matt. 28:15). They very likely feared reprisals from both the Jewish leaders and Pilate if they did otherwise. They sacrificed their own consciences for the sake of the material gain they received (cf. 1 Tim. 6:9-10). Matthew concluded his account of this matter by stating, "This story was widely spread among the Jews, and is to this day" (Matt. 28:15). More than likely it was the Jewish leaders who took pains to circulate this false rumor, demonstrating by their actions the "ungodliness and unrighteousness of men who suppress the truth in unrighteousness" (Rom. 1:18). The motive and method of their actions to discredit the reality of Christ's resurrection has been imitated and reproduced by unbelievers in different ways many times since that day. We are indebted to God, who guided Matthew to include this account in his Gospel, for unmasking this first hoax about Christ's resurrection in the light of the truth.

Christianity's Gibraltar: Christ's Resurrection

RICHARD L. MAYHUE

One Easter season during a trip to the Holy Land, Dr. Will Houghton (former president of Moody Bible Institute, 1934-1947) watched a large crowd march in the street. At the front of the procession, he saw a life-sized wax figure of Christ on the cross.

Mothers were holding up their children and saying, "Kiss the Christ! Kiss the Christ!"

Houghton became sickened by the hollow mockery. "It's a lie," he thought, "a base, terrible lie! He is not dead! The cross and the tomb are past! He is alive forevermore!"

Paul wrote to the confused Corinthians, "For I delivered to you as of first importance what I also received that Christ died for our sins according to the Scriptures, and that He was buried, and that He was raised on the third day according to the Scriptures" (1 Cor. 15:3-4).

God has provided many infallible proofs verifying Christ's triumph over death. The resurrection is the foundation for Christianity's exclusive claim that "no other name under heaven … has been given among men by which we must be saved" (Acts 4:12). What are those proofs?

Old Testament Scripture

"All things which are written about Me in the Law of Moses and the Prophets and the Psalms must be fulfilled," Jesus told His disciples. "Thus it is written, that the Christ would suffer and rise again from the dead the third day" (Luke 24:44, 46).

He certainly had Psalm 16:10 in mind: "For You will not abandon my soul to Sheol; Nor will You allow Your Holy One to undergo decay." Peter (Acts 2:25-28) and Paul (Acts 13:35) both preached Christ's resurrection from this psalm.

Old Testament Scriptures anticipated Messiah's resurrection one thousand years in advance.

Christ's Own Testimony

Each of the four Gospel writers included the Lord's predictions that He would die but rise again. "From that time Jesus began to show His disciples that He must go to Jerusalem, and suffer many things ... and be killed, and be raised up on the third day" (Matt. 16:21; also Mark 9:9; Luke 9:22; John 2:19). Even His enemies testified before Pilate, "Sir, we remember that when He was still alive that deceiver said, 'After three days I am to rise again'" (Matt. 27:63). Not only did David prophesy the resurrection in Psalm 16, but Jesus also unmistakably announced it.

Empty Tomb

What do Buddha, Confucius, Mohammed, Joseph Smith, and Karl Marx all have in common? If signs marked gravesites, theirs would read, "Occupied."

Only Christ's tomb rates a vacant sign. He arose on the third day, just as He said (Matt. 28:6; Mark 16:6; Luke 24:6; John 20:6-9). The empty tomb authenticates His resurrection.

Christ's Silent Enemies

The Savior's enemies never built a case against His resurrection. If reasonable doubt had existed, they would have seized the opportunity.

The chief priests fabricated a story that while the soldiers slept, Jesus' disciples stole His body (Matt. 28:11-15). How could they know who stole the body when the only witnesses were asleep?

In Acts, the Sadducees forbade the apostles to preach the resurrection (4:1-2, 17-18; 5:28). Why this prohibition if the resurrection never occurred? Because if they could not disprove the actual fact thereof, they could at least deny its proclamation.

Christ's Appearances after the Resurrection

The Lord Jesus appeared on at least ten separate occasions before a multitude of witnesses after He arose.

He showed Himself alive to Mary Magdalene (Mark 16:9), other women (Matt. 28:8-10), Peter (Luke 24:34), two on the Emmaus road (Luke 24:13-35), ten disciples (John 20:19-23), eleven disciples (John 20:26-29), seven disciples in Galilee (John 21:1-23), five hundred followers (1 Cor. 15:6), James (1 Cor. 15:7), and the Eleven at the ascension (Acts 1:3-11). Masses of people affirmed His resurrection.

Birth of the Church

God's Spirit could come only if Christ arose and ascended to heaven (John 16:7; Acts 1:8; 2:4), and Jesus instructed the apostles to wait for power from on high (Acts 1:4-5).

Pentecost would have been impossible if the Lord had not risen earlier. Christ's church has annually celebrated His resurrection (Easter) for almost two millennia.

Apostles' Witness

The major theme of the apostles' preaching was Christ's resurrection. They must have sounded to some like a broken record. Resurrection preaching dominates the entire book of Acts. Peter proclaimed it (2:32; 3:15; 5:30; 10:40), and so did Paul (13:30; 17:18, 31; 28:31). The apostles, honorable and trustworthy men, unanimously acclaimed the resurrection.

New Worship Day

The early church revered the first day of the week as unique. On that day, Christ met His disciples in a new intimacy of fellowship (John 20:19) and gave them instruction (Luke 24:1, 36-49). He ascended into heaven as the "firstfruits," or wave sheaf (Lev. 23:10-12; John 20:17; 1 Cor. 15:20, 23), and breathed the Spirit on them for a special commission (John 20:22). On the first day of the week, the Spirit descended from heaven (Acts 2:1-4).

The apostle Paul preached on the first day of the week (Acts 20:6-7). Believers came together to break bread on the first day and to give as God prospered them (1 Cor. 16:2).

Christian worship was changed from the seventh day to the first to celebrate Christ's resurrection. The day he rose (Matt. 28:1) reminds Christians weekly of the Lord's victory over death.

New Testament Scripture

The New Testament speaks more than one hundred times of our Lord's resurrection. Most convincing are His post-ascension appearances.

Stephen saw Christ standing at the Father's right hand (Acts 7:56). The Lord stood at Paul's side in Jerusalem (Acts 23:11). The beloved disciple, John, turned to see Him in the midst of seven golden lampstands (Rev 1:12).

It is a truth incontestably supported by the entire New Testament.

Paul's Conversion

During the nineteenth century, Lord Lyttleton and Gilbert West tried to discredit Christianity by disproving Paul's conversion and Christ's resurrection. After examining the facts, both of these outstanding leaders confessed Him as Savior and Lord.

Lyttleton realized that the church's most ardent persecutor really did have a personal confrontation with the resurrected Lord (Acts 9:1-22; 22:6-21; 26:4-23).

Symbolic Sacrament

Paul received instructions for the Lord's Table personally from the resurrected Christ (1 Cor. 11:23). The bread and cup regularly remind believers of the Lord's death until He comes (1 Cor. 11:26). Only the resurrection allows Him to ascend to the Father and return to gather His own.

Christian Doctrine

If the resurrection proves false, Christianity collapses. The resurrection is essential to the gospel "that Christ died for our sins according to the Scriptures, and that He was buried, and that He was raised on the third day according to the Scriptures" (1 Cor. 15:3-4).

Paul argued that without the resurrection, his preaching and the Corinthians' faith would be in vain (1 Cor. 15:14). He would even consider himself a false witness, the Corinthians would still be in their sins, and deceased loved ones would have perished without hope (vv. 15-18). If Christ had not risen from the dead, Christians, of all people, should be pitied (v. 19).

Salvation Message

Claiming to be a Christian while denying the resurrection is a contradiction of God's message to the church. "If you confess with your mouth Jesus as Lord, and believe in your heart that God raised Him from the dead, you shall be saved" (Rom. 10:9-10).

The resurrection of Jesus Christ cannot be divorced from believing and receiving His gift of eternal life. Paul inseparably linked the resurrection to salvation.

The Church's Historical Confession

Clement of Rome wrote about AD 96, "Let us understand, dearly beloved, how the Master continually showeth unto us the resurrection that shall be hereafter; whereof He made the Lord Jesus Christ the firstfruit, when He raised Him from the dead."[1]

The historic Westminster Confession (1647) reads, "On the third day he arose from the dead, with the same body in which he suffered; with which also he ascended into heaven, and there sitteth at the right hand of his Father."[2]

Famed historian Thomas Arnold (1795–1842) observed,

> The evidence of our Lord's life, and death, and resurrection, is of the same sort as that which we rest on in human matters. Whoever has heard the summing up of a judge on any great trial, will be able to understand what I mean; the jury have heard a great many witnesses; some of them have perhaps contradicted others, some have stated things very improbable; in a long cause, if the jury are unaccustomed to what are called the laws or rules of evidence, they may be utterly puzzled what to be-

---

[1] 1 Clement 24.

[2] Westminster Confession of Faith 8.4

lieve. But it is their business to pass a judgment in the matter, and therefore they must make up their minds one way or the other. In order to do this they are glad to listen to the summing up of the judge. He goes clearly through all the mass of evidence which seemed so contradictory and perplexing; he gives them reasons why such a witness is to be believed rather than another, how he had better means of knowing the truth, and less temptation to depart from it; how his evidence is in itself consistent when examined carefully, and has a look of truth about it; and so he shows the jury that they have very good grounds for making up their minds, and for giving their verdict. Now in the same way, the evidence of our Lord's life and death and resurrection, may be, and often has been shown to be, satisfactory; it is good according to the common rules for distinguishing good evidence from bad. Thousands and ten thousands of persons have gone through it piece by piece as carefully as ever judge summed up on a most important cause: I have myself done it many times over, not to persuade others, but to satisfy myself. I have been used for many years to study the history of other times, and to examine and weigh the evidence of those who have written about them; and I know of no one fact in the history of mankind, which is proved by better and fuller evidence of every sort to the understanding of a fair inquirer, than the great sign which God has given us, that Christ died and rose again from the dead.[3]

---

[3] Thomas Arnold, *Christian Life, Its Hopes, Its Fears, and Its Close*, 6th ed. (London: T. Fellowes, 1859), 14-16.

The resurrection evidence overwhelmingly proves that Jesus Christ did indeed gloriously rise from the dead the third day, just as He said He would. Thus, Christians worship a risen and living Lord Jesus Christ.

www.ingramcontent.com/pod-product-compliance
Lightning Source LLC
Chambersburg PA
CBHW060239050426
42448CB00009B/1516